Spiritual Perception

& Awareness

Recognizing Doctrines of Devils

Charlie P. Johnston Jr.

The Scriptures used throughout this book are quoted from the King James Version of the Bible. The author has taken the liberty to update some of the obsolete language used in this translation.

Published by: Johnston Publications

3667 Northside Church Road

Greenwood, FL 32443

(850) 592-8769

cjohnston464@gmail.com

ISBN:979-8-218-96244-9

Published 2023 - Printed in the United States of America

Dedication

This book is dedicating to the Community of Christian believers who are born-again of God's spirit.

My hope is:

- That they can become enlightened and encouraged to face up to the evil doctrines with which they are confronted.

- That they will be courageous in resisting the devil, and its dark doctrines.

- That they will learn to walk in the efficacy of God's power and presence in their lives.

Praise God for the opportunity to manifest the spiritual power He's placed within us!

Acknowledgment

This book would not have been written without the loving help of my one and only Carol Ann Johnston. She supported my ever effort in completing this book. What a wonderful, giving, wife she's been to me for over forty-four years. Praise God. My sons, Charlie P. Johnston III, and Timothy James Johnston worked through the manuscript to make suggestions and improvements. Helpful friends read the manuscript and offered their suggestions, among who are Gary and Becky Sheirer and Dave Duris.

CONTENTS

CONTENTS

PREFACE

Unless otherwise noted Scriptures quoted are from the King James version of the Bible. The author has taken the liberty to update some of the obsolete language used in this translation. Words such as thee and thou and others are replaced with more modern language.

This book is written with the resolve that God's Word can be trusted over and above any man's word. The author also believes the Bible (God's Word) is the only reliable foundation for life and living. Every diligent honest searching of the Bible will produce meaningful answers. Consequently, this book should appeal to Christian believers who love the Bible and Its contents. This work is offered to the serious hearted believer that is willing to investigate its contents and be challenged to change their thinking when it is necessary. The purpose of this book is to beckon the readers to carefully examine commonly accepted doctrinal beliefs; beliefs that are crafted with devilish intent. These sordid belief systems are contrary to the health and well being of our society and the way we are governed. These deceiving belief systems are at work against our morality and freedom. This is why we must carefully examine them one-by-one.

They must absolutely be exposed for the danger they pose. The light and truth of godly judgment must be directed upon these vicious and misleading falsehoods. All of these lying devilish doctrines need to be laid bare before the eyes of our citizenry and the political leadership controlling our government.

INTRODUCTION

The first three chapters of this book seek to describe the spiritual powers that affect all of our lives. Those who understand these powers and how they function are in a far better position to respond appropriately. Ignorance and denial about these powers can lead to the catastrophic loss of health, prosperity, and even one's life. On the other hand, to respond to these spiritual powers with understanding, and meek heartedness to learn, can bring peace, health, prosperity, and fulfillment to any individual.

In the first chapter we will see how God designed human life to consist of body, soul, and spirit. The lose of a spiritual nature occurred when Adam and Eve disobeyed their Creator. We will also see how God made the restoration of spirit life available through the ministry of Jesus Christ. With the empowerment of holy spirit life within them, Christian believers are now able to manifest their God-given abilities. Each of these nine spiritual abilities are fully described.

The second chapter describes the emptiness of human life devoid of spiritual understanding. With the lack of a spiritual compass men and women are limited to their five senses perception of life. Their history

3

reveals an inability to get along with each other. We will see how their limited knowledge keeps them ignorant of demonic powers. They remain dull in their understanding of God. Their remedy is to turn to the Lord Jesus Christ for deliverance and salvation. Their biggest need is to become born-again of God's spirit.

The third chapter reveals the nature and character of the devil by a study of its biblical names. We will take note of this evil spirit's attempt to replace Almighty God. By the end of this chapter we should be able to identify many of the devil's characteristics, and how its method is to steal, kill, and destroy.

Chapters four through eight show how several commonly accepted beliefs, are in reality, false doctrines. They are cleverly designed falsehoods that are, in fact, counterfeits of truth. In reality, these beliefs are doctrines of devils. The devil has dug a dangerous pit; the gullible and unsuspecting will fall therein.

I Peter 5:8-9

Be sober, be vigilant; because your adversary the devil, as a roaring lion, walks about, seeking whom he may devour: who resist steadfast in the faith, knowing that the same afflictions are accomplished in your brethren that are in the world.

The five wayward doctrines are: possession or choice, transgender lies, the climate change hoax, the dead are alive and in heaven, and the doctrine of the Trinity.

An extended summary seeks to reinforce the main teachings presented throughout the book.

CHAPTER 1

SPIRIT LIFE

One way to understand the circumstances surrounding men and women living on planet Earth is to establish the presence or absence of spirit life in them. It's obvious that human life had a physical beginning. Our ancestry proves that. So here we are actively living and working and playing and dancing and whatever else we choose to do with ourselves. But what about our spiritual nature? We surely need to understand all we can about its presence or the absence thereof. The complete meaning of our lives is what we need to know. There are many views about the origin of human life and its ultimate purpose and how it is to function best. In the following pages, we are going to consider two of these views, and how the spiritual aspect of life fits into them. First, we will look into the biblical view.

THE BIBLICAL VIEW

God has defined Himself! He has defined Himself to be an Eternal Spirit. The Lord Jesus Christ said of God, (John 4:24) "God is a Spirit:

and they that worship Him must worship Him in spirit and in truth." Spirit life exists beyond the dimension of our five senses' perception; consequently, we can only know what God has revealed to us about Himself. Even though God is spirit He has defined Himself to have the characteristics of a father. This is why God can rightfully be referred to as a He. His behavior toward us is like that of a good human father who nurtures and provides for his children. When Jesus taught his disciples how to pray he referred to God as "our Father" in heaven. So then, the pronoun "He" is rightfully used in reference to God Almighty.

God chose to speak His creation into existence by the use of words. Words are in the dimension of the five senses. We who are His creation understand words. That is, of course, how we communicate with each other. But, it is also how God communicates with us and we with Him. Words transcend the gulf between heaven and earth. We can hear the words that God speaks to us, and God hears the words of our prayers. The book of Genesis describes for us how God, in the beginning, created the heavens and the earth. It explains that God literally spoke His creation into being. What He spoke came to pass. God said, "Let there be" and it became.1 That is exactly how the heavens and the earth, and all that is therein came to be.

The qualities and attributes of God are limitless. Being Spirit, God is without a beginning or an end. He possesses omnipotent power; and as our loving Heavenly Father, He's always good. He's faithful and truthful; we can count on what He says He will do. He's omnipresent, that is, His presence is not limited to time and space. He's omniscient, that is, He's all-knowing. He hears our prayers. He also has foreknowledge; He can see what will come to pass before it comes to pass. He is invisible to the human eye, and He is, in all aspects, perfect and holy. He remains sovereign over all His creation. He is also righteous and worthy of our worship. He's a merciful and gracious God who forgives sin. He is the Giver of Life and the Savior of man. The Earth and the Universe are a reflection of His magnificent power and beauty. God is unlimited in scope and purpose. His greatness no one can fathom. The prophet Moses requested that God show to him His glory; But that was more than Moses could behold. 2

BODY, SOUL, AND SPIRIT MAN

The next thing we are going to do is look at God's awesome design and makeup of man as is recorded in Genesis chapters 1 and 2.

Genesis 1:27

So God created man in His own image, in the image of God created He him; male and female created He them.

Genesis 2:7

And the Lord God formed man of the dust of the ground and breathed into his nostrils the breath of life; and man became a living soul.

The man God first created had a physical body and a soul. Soul life is breath life. It entails taking in oxygen and expelling carbon dioxide. Without "breath life" a man dies. (We'll treat the aspect of the "spirit of man" in the next chapter.) God also included in man's makeup "holy spirit life." Remember, God is Spirit and when He created man in His own image He gave man "holy spirit life." So, the first man's (Adam's) makeup included body, soul, and holy spirit. Having "holy spirit life" enabled Adam to communicate with God and God with him. He and God were on a first-name basis, so-to-speak. There were no breaches between them. The channels of understanding between them were first-rate. God was able to teach the holy spirit He had given Adam and then Adam's holy spirit could teach his mind. This was the communication process God intended. God taught Adam, via his holy spirit, what he should do and also what he should not do. The one restriction God gave Adam was the following:

Genesis 2:15-17

And the Lord God took the man and put him into the Garden of Eden to dress it and to keep it. And the Lord God commanded the man, saying, of every tree of the garden you may freely eat: But of the tree of the knowledge of good and evil, you shall not eat of it: for in the day that you eat thereof you shall surely die.

Before Adam and his wife Eve participated in eating that forbidden fruit they knew no evil. However, in disobedience to God, they chose to eat of that forbidden fruit. The consequence of their rebellious behavior against God restricted them to a body and soul existence. They became limited to only their five senses knowledge; taste, touch, sight, smell, and hearing. They lost their holy spiritual nature, it died.

8

Adam then became a natural man of only body and soul. The following verse of Scripture makes it clear that spiritual communication with God requires Spirit-to-spirit action.

I Corinthians 2:14

But the natural man receives not the things of the Spirit of God: for they are foolishness unto him: neither can he know them, because they are SPIRITUALLY discerned.

THE REBIRTH OF SPIRIT LIFE

The prodigy of Adam and Eve were men and women whose make-up was only body and soul life; they were without holy spirit. This was true of men and women throughout the Old Testament period. However, our loving Heavenly Father has provided a way for men and women to regain holy spirit life. He has given the world a Savior, the Lord Jesus Christ, who is King of Kings and Lord of Lords. The means by which men and women can regain holy spirit life is by the accomplishments of Jesus Christ. Jesus lived a perfect life before God, his Heavenly Father. Jesus taught people by mighty signs, miracles, and wonders to trust their Heavenly Father. Jesus always looked to God for His guidance and His power, so that he might bless God's people and bring deliverance to their lives. He also taught his nation to honor God by obeying His will.

Jesus Christ became the perfect sacrifice for sin. He paid the price for the sins of his people and the people of the world. He secured the forgiveness of sins by the shedding of his sinless blood. He willingly laid down his life in obedience to his Heavenly Father knowing that His Father would raise him from the pain of death. His obedience to God secured the means by which men and women can get born-again of God's spirit. After Jesus Christ had completed his awesome mighty works, God raised him from the dead and made him the Lord of Life.

The simplicity of how men and women can be spiritually born-again of God's spirit is presented to us by the following verses of Scripture.

John 3:16-17

For God so loved the world, that He gave His only begotten son, that whosoever believes in him should not perish, but have everlasting life. For God sent not His son into the world to condemn the world, but that the world through him might be saved.

Romans 10:9-10

That if you shall confess with your mouth the Lord Jesus and shall believe in your heart that God has raised him from the dead, you shall be saved. For with the heart man believes unto righteousness and with the mouth confession is made unto salvation.

The very instant an individual believes in their heart-of-hearts that God raised Jesus Christ from the dead, and confesses the reality that Jesus Christ has become the Lord of their life, they receive holy spirit life. The miracle of all miracles has occurred for that individual. They are no longer a body and soul man restricted to their five senses understanding. Now they have God's gift to them, the gift of holy spirit. They have become complete in their makeup. They are the way God originally made the first man, Adam. The spiritual gift they have received becomes integrated into their entire body makeup. Spirit life has become a living vital part of them. God is Spirit and He has given them of His spirit. They have received the spiritual gift of the living God, living within them. He lives within them to teach and guide their lives.

SPIRITUAL QUALITIES

It does take a while for newborn babes in Christ to get acquainted with the spiritual life that now is alive within them. They must realize that their new spirit does not control them. Instead, they need to learn how to operate the gift they have received from their Heavenly Father. They must control their new spirit, it does not control them. This is very important information because misguided doctrines in the Christian community have taught that the holy spirit will take control of a person. This is not true! Our Heavenly Father never controls us. He has given us freedom of will so that we can choose to obey and love Him. This is a hard and fast rule. A person always has freedom of choice. The responsibility to love God and to obey Him rests upon every Christian's shoulders. "We love God because He first loved us". What a Savior!

When the new birth of spirit occurs in us, it comes loaded with supernatural abilities. These abilities are new to us and we must learn to operate them through growth and practice. Remember that we control them, they do not control us. A good analogy here is a reference to the way an automobile operates. Automobiles have horns, headlights, brake lights, radios, heaters, and many other functions. However, none of these functions will operate in an automobile until the key is turned on and the power to run them is supplied. Then the horn can be honked, and the radio can be played.

None of the abilities that come with our new spiritual nature will be visibly activated until we initiate them. We bring them into an active performance. When the believer fails to act, he will not manifest his gift. It is only when the individual believes to operate his God-given ability that he can bring it into evidence. God gives the gift, but it is the individual believer's responsibility to manifest it; to bring it into action.

THE NINE GOD-GIVEN POWERS OF A SPIRIT- FILLED LIFE

Nine of these awesome spiritual abilities are listed for us in the New Testament.3 They are named as follows: word of wisdom, word of knowledge, faith, gifts of healing, working of miracles, prophecy, discerning of spirits, unknown tongues, the interpretation of tongues. The following paragraphs will treat each one of these spiritual abilities individually, but will present them in a different order.

The operation of these nine manifestations of holy spirit will be new to those who read about them for the first time. Please don't get bogged down! God designed the simplicity of all these spiritual abilities so that every believer can benefit by them. They are not complex. They are natural and easy to operate when they are understood. So, please take sufficient time to gain the understanding you need. Soon you will be operating them like a champion in your daily life. Remember that God does the speaking and you do the listening. The endowment of our spiritual nature has armed us with supernatural, miraculous, power. We should, and must, live our lives in the glory of that great reality.4

The outstanding power of the gift of holy spirit enables the Christian believers to manifest God's presence at work within them. The new believer can learn to look to God in all things. This should become the way they live their lifes. They can learn to listen to what their Heavenly Father teaches, and also the importance of performing that which is revealed to them. They simply listen expectedly to their Heavenly Father and act upon the information they have received from Him.

There are nine God-given spiritual powers that work together harmoniously. Word of knowledge and word of wisdom are companion manifestations. Their operation is exclusive of our five senses human knowledge. In the action of the word of knowledge, God gives unique information to the individual believer. The information one receives from God will bring enlightenment and help in a given situation. The message one receives from God can be extensive or simply a few words.

God is in no way limited in the way He presents His word of knowledge; it's Spirit-to-spirit communication. He tailor-makes His message to the individual's capacity to receive. Again, the process by which it works is God speaks to the spirit He has given an individual, and the individual's spirit then instructs their mind. The individual believer can then act upon the message they have received from God. It is their action upon the message from God that becomes the performance of the word of wisdom. They have the knowledge God has given them, and they literally perform it. They act upon it and bring about the profit needed. By the operation of the word of knowledge and the word of wisdom, the believer is empowered. They are empowered to meet their unique needs but also the unique needs of other groups and individuals.

The utilization of the word of knowledge and the word of wisdom are essential in operating the manifestation of the discerning of spirits. In the operation of discerning of spirits, God may reveal to you the necessary information concerning the presence or non-presence of spirits. He can teach you the identity of the spirit that may be present in an individual. This is His option; if He doesn't give the information there's nothing to receive. God is the expert in the spirit realm. He decides to give the information and the individual believer decides to receive it. He may reveal to you the spiritual state of an individual born-again from on high. He may also identify to you the presence of evil spirits and if you are to cast them out in the name of Jesus Christ. This manifestation enables believers to bring deliverance to their brethren and other individuals who have been tricked and hindered by their adversary, the devil. The love of God in the heart of Christian believers motivates them to bring deliverance to those possessed by evil spirits.

So, it is easy to see the operation of word of knowledge and word of wisdom are at work together in discerning of spirits. Word of knowledge teaches believers the necessary information concerning the spirits that may be present, and word of wisdom teaches them what to do about it. If evil spirits are present the believer is told whether or not to cast them out. To cast out evil spirits also involves two additional manifestations; the manifestation of believing faith and the working of a miracle. Next, we are going to look at these two wonderful manifestations and how they operate harmoniously with the discerning of spirits.

The manifestation of faith can be defined as believing faith. This is true because faith is the operation of belief. The manifestation of faith is the God-given ability to believe for the impossible to come to pass. It comes to pass according to the believer's acting upon the message God gives them. The words one is to speak are based upon the information the individual has received by word of knowledge and word of wisdom. The believer can then literally speak for the impossible to come to pass by his or her own command. God has taught the believer what he or she is to do in a particular situation and the words that one is to speak to bring a miracle of deliverance to pass.

The performing of a miracle is the God-given ability to speak into existence acts that may be contrary to natural laws. The laws of nature may be superseded by the spoken word of a born-again believer. These miraculous acts are performed to bring deliverance to God's people. Additionally, they can influence the natural man of body and soul. Since miracles are performed out in the natural world those who behold them can be inspired to believe in the power and deliverance of Almighty God. They see His mighty works and may begin to believe that these mighty works are by the hand of our loving Heavenly Father.

The next manifestation of the spirit we are going to talk about is the gifts of healing. Please notice that the word "gifts" is plural. It's plural because, when necessary, the gifts of healing can be utilized over and over again to bring health and healing to the individual seeking it. When God reveals the necessary information about the individual's needs, they can be ministered to in the name of Jesus Christ. If no specific words come from God about the individual who needs healing the best that can be done for that person is prayer. The one ministering can pray according to their understanding. When there is sufficient belief, prayer can get the job done.

When the individual seeking healing is healed instantly, then a miracle has occurred. Now by this time, you can clearly see that word of knowledge, word of wisdom, discerning of spirits, and believing for miracles, are all a part of the healing manifestation. All of the processes that bring healing and deliverance to those who are seeking it are from God. It's God's working, He does the work! And yes, the marvelous simplicity of how all this works is that we just listen to what God tells us and we then speak it into action. What we speak is absolutely going to come to pass; yes, even signs, miracles, and wonders for all to behold.

Oh, what a joy and privilege it is to speak words of healing deliverance to men and women, boys and girls. We do this by the power of God working in us! We need to stay busy doing the works of our Heavenly Father. It is when we are working for God that our spiritual abilities will come to the foreground. When we are teaching the unsaved how to get born-again, when we are ministering to the sick, when we are proclaiming the gospel of our Lord Jesus Christ, and when we are supporting and inspiring fellow believers, God will supply the information needed to get the job done. God will give us the words that help us to reconcile men and women back to Him. This is the ministry He has given us, and we have the spiritual ability to bring it to pass.

Now we have gotten to the God-given spiritual ability of speaking in tongues (you, the believer, can speak a language unknown to yourself). Speaking in tongues is the performance of spiritual power. The depth of this ability is outstanding; it's absolutely amazing! Born-again believers may exercise this God-given ability whenever they choose to do so. However, if they choose to speak in tongues in a believer's worship service then they should also believe to operate the companion manifestation of the interpretation of tongues. To speak in tongues openly before a group of people who do not understand the language being spoken is not profitable for that group. It is true that on special occasions an individual who may be present in the group of believers can understand the language being spoken in tongues. This is true because speaking in tongues is either the language of men, or it can be the language of angels. We will discuss the interpretation of tongues a little later.

Speaking in tongues is proof positive that you have been given spiritual life. Your spirit enables you. You control it, it does not control you. You, by your own will, can speak forth openly, out into the world of the senses, the evidence of your amazing ability. You can speak this God-given language in the same way you speak the language you normally speak. Not even the devil can duplicate this wonderful ability. It cannot supply an ability it does not possess.

Speaking in tongues can be practiced by the believer in one's private prayer life, or while one is at work, and even at play. Generally speaking, there are no restrictions on when you speak. The more speaking in tongues is practiced the better. Even the Apostle Paul said that he spoke in tongues more than the believers in the Corinthian Church. The benefits of this amazing ability go on and on.

The following is a partial list of this fruitful activity:

Speaking in tongues is proof that the spirit of God lives in you. It is proof that the resurrection of Jesus Christ is true, it's a reality. It's the assurance that you are born-again from above. Whenever you need to know that the presence of God is in your life, speak in tongues; it confirms His presence. It sensitizes and enlarges your understanding of God's power and presence within you.

Speaking in tongues brings rest and peace to your life. Even in the middle of a troubled world, you can remain peaceful and at ease. It closes out the troubles of the world, and a troubled mind, and brings restfulness to your life.

Speaking in tongues strengthen your inner spiritual man. It increases your spiritual capacity. Your ability to discern spiritual matters increases and grows. It magnifies God's presence in your life.

Speaking in tongues is perfect prayer and praise.

Romans 8:26

Likewise, the spirit also helps our infirmities; for we know not what we should pray for as we ought: but the spirit itself makes intercession for us with groanings that cannot be uttered.

It is certainly true that you do not always know what you should pray for. However, this manifestation provides the ultimate assistance to your prayers because it enables perfect prayer. Praying in tongues never misses, and it is always pleasing to God. And yes, God is always worthy of your praise. How wonderful and settling it is that you can praise Him perfectly even with groanings that you cannot normally utter. There are many other golden benefits to speaking in tongues; however, it is not within the scope of this book to treat each one individually. The benefits treated above should be a positive motivation for God's people to embrace speaking in tongues and practice it wholeheartedly.

The next manifestation of the spirit we are going to discuss is the interpretation of tongues. It is the performance of a spiritual power. It's miraculous! Speaking in tongues is a message spoken to God. However, in a believers' meeting the interpretation of tongues is a message from God to God's people, the church. It is the God-given ability to bring forth the interpretation of the unknown language you have just spoken to a gathering of believers. The interpretation will be in the language of the people present so that they can understand it. The interpretation that is given will be a message of edification for the church; comforting words. They will be words that encourage believers to a worthier endeavor. The message is inspired utterance from the speaker. The interpreted words are given to the speaker as one begins to speak them forth to the hearers. The speaker trusts that God is giving him or her the message and they are speaking it forth enthusiastically. God is always faithful! Those who hear this message from God are edified immensely. God's message will encourage His people to be their best.

The last of these nine spiritual abilities we're going to discuss is the manifestation of prophecy. Its purpose is to bring a message from God for the edification of the church. If all in the church are fully instructed this manifestation bypasses the speaking of unknown tongues and the interpretation thereof. Rather, the believer speaking brings forth directly word-by-word the message he or she is given from God. The believer who is speaking, speaks because he or she is inspired to speak from a loving heart and a desire to bless God's people. God speaks to the speaker's spirit and that spirit teaches one's mind. The message given is for the believers who are gathered for that occasion.

There needs to be some clarity between the manifestation of prophecy and the gift ministry of a prophet. The manifestation of prophecy is different from the gift ministry of a prophet. The gift ministry of a prophet is God's gift to the body of Christian believers;

those who make up the church. God selects the individuals best suited to function in this capacity and empowers them to perform the work of a prophet. The ministry of a prophet is given to men and women who can bring new light to their day and time. They are called by God to do so. A prophet acts like a mouthpiece to bless God's people. God reveals to the prophet, by revelation, the message one is to deliver. Indeed, a prophet may occasionally foretell what will come to pass in the message he or she is delivering. Generally, however, the message of the prophet deals with the present condition of God's people. If they need repentance he or she speaks to that need. If the people are turning away from God and practicing idolatry he or she speaks to that need. If God's people are seeking deliverance the message from the prophet will speak to that need. However, in the manifestation of prophecy, any born-again believer who has been instructed and desires to manifest his spiritual ability can bring forth a word of prophecy to those present in a believers' assembly.

VICTORIOUS LIVING

God has empowered His people through the rebirth of their spiritual nature. They are enabled to live far above the onslaughts of an evil and corrupt world.5 Praise God! They are empowered by the excellency of the holy spirit they have received. The operating of their spiritual abilities brings healing and deliverance to God's people, and also to those who are ready to get born-again from above. Spirit-filled men and women can walk victoriously with the presence of God directing their lives. The spirit of God within them is as close as the air they breathe. They can speak with Him in perfect prayer and praise. The rebirth of holy spirit life in men and women makes them complete. They are completely complete! They are no longer confined to a five sense's body and soul existence. They can live victoriously. The promise of life hereafter in a new spiritual body belongs to them. God is their present help. God is their companion. He's there to meet their needs. He's their constant supply. It is their loving Heavenly Father who is their strength and He's their sure reward.

In the next chapter, we will begin to look more closely at the natural man whose makeup is only body and soul. The contrast between the natural man and the spiritual man should become fully evident.

1 See Genesis 1:3

2 Exodus 33:18-ff

3 See I Corinthians 12:1-31

4 Victor Paul Wiereville's book, *Receiving The Holy Spirit Today*, has an outstanding treatment of this subject.

5 See Ephesians 3:14-21

CHAPTER 2

THE SECOND VIEW – LIFE WITHOUT HOLY SPIRIT

The natural-man is defined biblically as one having the absence of holy spirit life. His makeup is that of a body and a soul. Soul life is breathe life, but it entails more than the ability to breathe. The natural man of body and soul includes "the spirit of man." It is the spirit of man that generates his capacity; what he is potentially capable of; what he is able to do. The spirit of man is the inner seat of what he thinks, his emotions, and his desires. These are all aspects of his personality by which he establishes his will. His will is what he chooses to do or to believe. The spirit of man is not what mankind lost in the Garden of Eden. What he lost was eternal life, holy spirit. The holy spirit life by which Adam communicated with God no longer lived within him; it ceased to be.[1] This is why biblically, natural-man is referred to as a man of body and soul.

I Corinthians 2:14

But the natural man receives not the things of the Spirit of God: for they are foolishness unto him: neither can he know them, because they are spiritually discerned.

We are not going to see a rosy picture as we begin to look into the life of a natural-man of flesh and blood. The spirit of man seeks to live forever, but his sinful rebellion against God has made death the penalty he must face. Without a spiritual connection with God, men and women are in the "soup," so-to-speak. Their wisdom is earth-bound. They are referred to biblically as walking after the flesh.

Romans 8:5-7

For they that are after the flesh do mind the things of the flesh; but they that are after the Spirit the things of the Spirit. For to be carnally minded is death; but to be spiritually minded is life and peace. Because the carnal mind is enmity against God: for it is not subject to the law of God, neither indeed can be.

The dimension of holy spirit life is beyond their understanding. Often they are like the blind leading the blind. They fail to acknowledge that which God made them to be. Consequently, they search for meaning about themselves. They fail to see the divine purposes that God intended for them. Because of their short-sighted understanding, they are literally without hope and without God in the midst of a crooked, evil world. They remain callous to the things of God. They stumble through life seeking the treasures this world offers them.

I John 2:16-17

For all that is in the world, the lust of the flesh, and the lust of the eyes, and the pride of life, is not of the Father, but is of the world. And the world passes away, and the lust thereof: but he that does the will of God abides for ever.

What a sad indictment, but it's true. Natural-minded men and women, who are without holy spirit, seek to set their own standards. They try to decipher between right and wrong, good and bad, but they are limited to their earthbound understanding. They glory in the works of their hands but they fail to acknowledge the wonderful works of God. They often become indifferent towards God and ignore His existence.

With no regard for the True God's presence, natural-minded men and women, early on, began to build their own gods and kneeled before them with their worship. The practice of their pagan idolatry carried them farther and farther into corruption.

Genesis 6:5

And God saw that the wickedness of man was great in the earth, and that every imagination of the thoughts of his heart was only evil continually.

History reveals the tragic road natural-minded people of body and soul have traveled. The ancient historian, Josephus, describes a little about the process by which natural men and women rebelled against their Creator.

Now it was Nimrod who excited them (Noah's ancestry) to such an affront and contempt of God. He was the grandson of Ham, the son of Noah, a bold man, and of great strength of hand. He persuaded them (Noah's ancestry) not to ascribe it (their well-being) to God, as if it was through his (Nimrod's) means they were happy, but to believe that it was their own courage which procured that happiness. He also gradually changed the government into tyranny, seeing no other way of turning men from the fear of God, but to bring them into a constant dependence on his (Nimrod's) power. [2]

Before long, in their history, the ancient Babylonians had begun to worship a virtual pantheon of gods. In an attempt to explain the spiritual realities and forces affecting their lives, they worshipped the false gods they had made. Pagan nations throughout the history of the world have practiced destructive idolatry. What could be known of the true God they rejected.

Romans 1:20–23

For the invisible things of Him (God) from the creation of the world are clearly seen, being understood by the things that are made, even His eternal power and Godhead; so that they are without excuse: Because that, when they knew God, they glorified Him not as God, neither were thankful; but became vain in their imaginations, and their foolish heart was darkened. Professing themselves to be wise, they became fools, and changed the glory of the uncorruptible God into an image made like to corruptible man, and to birds, and four-footed beast, and creeping things.

FAILED LEADERSHIP

The dilemma of the natural-man is that he has ignored the ultimate checks and balances of God's Wonderful Word. God's rulership, the ideal way to rule people, they have rejected. The disastrous tragedies of how natural-minded people began to rule one another are evident. Their methods of governing became tyrannical. Throughout ancient history and up to the present day, natural-minded individuals have devised systems of rulership that are contrary to the people they try to govern. Oligarchy, monarchy, colonialism, communism, and dictatorships of many varieties are all representative of their totalitarian rulership. Their tyrannical forms of government have led directly to wars and rumors of wars.

Wars and rumors of wars have existed on planet Earth since the early days of human history. Who is it that doesn't know Cain killed his brother Abel? With the development of nations, hostilities soon erupted between them. A list of ancient wars is so extensive there's just no need to search all of them out. Some of the better-known wars between nations are the following: the ancient Assyrian defeated the Egyptians, the Babylonians defeated the Assyrians, the Persians defeated the Babylonians, the Greeks defeated the Persians, and Rome was destroyed by invading hordes from Asia. In the seventh century AD, the Muslims conquered most of the nations around the Mediterranean Sea. More modern wars include the American Revolution, the Indian Wars of North America, the Persian Wars, the European Wars, and, of course, World War I and II. This list is by no means extensive, as a matter of fact, it is rather a skimpy listing. Think about all those who have died in history as a result of natural-minded men and women's inability to live peaceably with each other. The historical record of natural men and women is bleak at best. War is only one of the things they've done to abuse themselves.

OTHER SHORTCOMINGS

The natural-minded have other serious shortcomings that need to be addressed. Many of their unethical standards allow room for lewd behaviors like homosexuality, group sex, and sex transformation operations. Those who participate in this kind of sordid behavior have closed their hearts off to the admonitions of the following verses of Scripture:

Romans 1:26-32

For this cause God gave them up unto vile affections: for even their women did change the natural use into that which is against nature: And likewise also the men, leaving the natural use of the woman, burned in their lust one toward another; men with men working that which is unseemly, and receiving in themselves that recompense of their error which was meet. And even as they did not like to retain God in their knowledge, God gave them over to a reprobate mind, to do those things which are not convenient: being filled with all unrighteousness, fornication, wickedness, covetousness, maliciousness; full of envy, murder, debate, deceit, malignity; whisperers, Backbiters, haters of God, despiteful, proud, boasters, inventors of evil things, disobedient to parents, without understanding, covenant breakers, without natural affection, implacable, unmerciful: Who knowing the judgment of God, that they which commit such things are worthy of death, not only do the same, but have pleasure in them that do them.

MISGUIDED ASSUMPTIONS

Another fallacy of individuals who operate their lives with only five senses knowledge (the natural-minded) is that they are prone to adopt false, unrealistic, doctrines. They actually may claim to be controlled by fate or chance.[3] They think the strange power of fate locks their lives into the inevitable, and the force of chance deals with them harshly. The blank spots in their thinking and beliefs have led them to erroneous conclusions. We are going to give a fuller account of their fatalistic thinking in a later chapter.

The egos of many natural-minded individuals have imagined vain things. They have justified the philosophies of men and women to guide the way they live and what they believe. However, the best of their philosophical teachings have never brought about deliverance from sin or the promise of eternal life.

Today an "if it feels good - do it" mentality is lodged in the minds of a great many of our natural-minded young people. They are not restrained by the commonsense values that are needed to govern themselves. Misinformed liberal teachers and professors have led them astray. Their instructors have instilled socialistic values into their thinking.

Our younger natural-minded generation now operates in key positions in business and government. They are using social media platforms to inject their unwholesome values and standards into our culture. They're negatively influencing our government. Many of their beliefs pertaining to how we should be governed are intrusive. They are seeking to replace our established rights. Their lack of a "godly standard of morality" reveals their misguided foundation. Maybe they are not qualified to establish righteous judgment in the laws that govern our nation!

Many natural-minded liberals think that their standards and values are the only valid ones. They do not allow any debate about it either. Their shortsighted stance has become a cancer, eating away the true values of our society and our society's government. Their elusive, shaky, doctrines are undermining the traditional way our government has performed since its inception. The impending need is that they are stopped in their tracks. Rightful leadership, by those filled with God's spirit, can bring about the much-needed changes. This will certainly require more than just talk. It will require the cleansing of our nation's sinful ways and a return to honoring God in the way we live our lives. The natural-mind is truly enmity against God.

DENIAL OF THE SPIRITUAL SPHERE OF LIFE

One of the biggest dilemmas natural-minded individuals have is their failure to recognize the existence of the devil and its evil works.[4] Sometimes they even joke about the possibility of its reality. In so doing, they have deprived themselves of the enlightening spiritual view of life. Their failure to comprehend spiritual phenomena seriously limits their understanding. They remain baffled in unbelief.

They also remain vulnerable to the consequences of the devil's devices. It's no wonder they are tossed about by every wind of doctrine. It is no wonder they end up with so many false conclusions. They claim that hurricanes and tornadoes, floods and earthquakes, sickness and death, are works of nature or worse yet, "acts of God." Their unfounded conclusions keep them in the dark about the spiritual forces that are actively maneuvering these matters. It is no wonder that natural-minded individuals are seriously inept when it comes to recognizing devilish doctrines.

RECEIVING SPIRIT LIFE

Although the avenue to become born-again of God's spirit was dealt with in the proceeding chapter, there are a few details that need to be highlighted here. The natural-minded have little room to boast about their accomplishments. Their earthbound works are works of the flesh and they will not endure. In the end, their works will turn to dust. Earth-bound life will not go on without end. Everyone must eventually deal with that reality. With death comes the corruption of earthly bodies. If that is all there is, who could describe a darker future? The philosophy and aspirations of men offer no hope or comfort about the stark reality of death. So, without holy spirit life, the natural-minded can see no further than the here-and-now. They fail to hope in life after death.

God is merciful and gracious. In spite of their unbelief He endowed the natural-minded with blessings and benefits. "For He makes His sun to rise on the evil and on the good, and sends rain on the just and on the unjust" (Matthew 5:45b). It is by His goodness that God calls men and women to wholeness. He has provided a means of deliverance from their sins and shortcomings. It is God "Who will have all men to be saved, and to come unto the knowledge of the truth" (I Timothy 2:4). His gracious love has always rained down upon His creation. He has provided the only pathway to everlasting life. The natural-minded may boast about their accomplishments. However, their earthbound works are works of the flesh.

I Corinthians 15: 50

Now this I say, brethern, that flesh and blood cannot inhert the kingdom of God; neither does corruption inhert incorruption.

I Corinthians 3:11-14

For other foundation can no man lay than that is laid, which is Jesus Christ. Now if any man build upon this foundation gold, silver, precious stones, wood, hay, stubble; every man's work shall be made manifest: for the day shall declare it, because it shall be revealed by fire; the fire shall try every man's work of what sort it is. If any man's work abide which he hath built thereupon, he shall receive a reward.

The dilemma of the natural-minded can change. They can begin to hope in God. By God's beckoning call, He has provided the means by which they can be delivered from sin and death. They can receive the marvelous gift of holy spirit life by turning to God in belief. The remedy to life without spirit is to receive the gospel of the Lord Jesus Christ with child-like believing. With meekness of heart, they can choose, by their freedom of will, to receive God's gift of salvation.

Matthew 11:28-30

Come unto me, all you that labor and are heavy laden, and I will give you rest. Take my yoke upon you, and learn of me; for I am meek and lowly in heart: and you shall find rest unto your souls. For my yoke is easy, and my burden is light.

God's wonderful plan of salvation has been extended to all of humanity. He desires that every living soul be saved from their sins and born-again of His spirit. Whenever anyone believes that God raised His son, Jesus Christ, from the dead, and they then make Jesus Christ the Lord of their life, they will have received everlasting life. They become born-again of God's spirit. They will have the power and presence of God's spirit born within them.

We are not through with our examination of spiritual entities. In the next chapter, we will begin to look into the reality of evil spirit life, and how to stand against it!

1 See Genesis 2:16-17

2 *The Life and Works of Flavius Josephus*, trans William Whiston and intro H. Stebbing, Holt, Rinehary and Winston, N.Y. p.39

3 Johnston, Charlie P., *No Such Thing as Luck*, Johnston Publications, Greenwood, FL, 2005, p.93ff

4 See Ephesians 2:2-3

CHAPTER 3

EVIL SPIRIT LIFE

The Bible describes a third spiritual entity, one that's hostile to God; and, an adversary to God's people. Though Bible translations refer to this spirit as a "he", please bear in mind that spirit has no gender and is therefore in no sense of the word a person. This spirit can more accurately be referred to by the pronoun "it." So, it might take a little discipline to think of this spirit as an "it" rather than a "he" but it will be profitable to do so.

The Scriptures teach of this spiritual entity's creation, its stupendous beauty, its rebellion against its Creator, and of its everlasting destruction. When God created this spirit it performed in the way He planned for it to behave; however, later that changed.

Ezekiel 28:15

You were perfect in your ways from the day that you were created, until iniquity was found in you.

God was not into puppetry! The perfection of this spiritual archangel included its having free will. This creature became evil when it chose,

34

by freedom of will, to rebel against its Creator:

Ezekiel 28:17a

Your heart was lifted up because of your beauty, you have corrupted your wisdom by reason of your brightness.

By its freedom of will it set about to destroy the true God and Father of our Lord Jesus Christ. Its desire and intent became to replace its Creator. Its works and purposes are all directed towards that end. This spirit's prideful, egocentric, ambition led to its downfall. Its arrogant rebellion against its Creator is truly indicative of its flawed evil nature.

Isaiah 14:12-13

How are you fallen from heaven, O Lucifer, son of the morning! How are you cut down to the ground, which did weaken the nations!

For you have said in your heart, I will ascend into heaven, I will exalt my throne above the stars of God: I will sit also upon the mount of the congregation, in the sides of the north.

THE DEVIL'S NAMES

Next we are going to look at some of the biblical names for this evil spirit. They are as followers: Lucifer, that old serpent, the tempter, the devil, Satan, the destroyer, an adversary, the thief, a dragon, and an enemy. By looking at the meaning of these various biblical names we can begin to understand the depths of its destructive purposes, its methods, and we shall also learn of its final absolute destruction.

LUCIFER

In its early biblical appearance, this spirit is referred to by the name Lucifer. The name itself means "bright star" or "morning star." Lucifer is depicted as an outstanding, beautiful, archangel. It's beauty is compared to precious stones. (Every precious stone was your covering. Ezekiel 28:13a) By reason of its appealing beauty Lucifer seeks to reveal itself and its purposes as an angel of light; none the less, its intent is always evil. In other words, it's a "wolf in sheep's clothing." Lucifer's purposes are presented as truth, but they are the opposite of truth. It takes the discerning of the spiritual-minded to recognize its ploys. Lucifer is described as being second only to God, its Creator. However, its rebellion against its Creator led directly to it being cast down to Earth, and completely out of the heavenly realm. When Lucifer was cast out of heaven it brought one-third of the angels with it. It's been an earth dweller ever since and its sphere of influence is limited to an earthly realm. The angel spirits under Lucifer's command do its bidding; this is why they are referred to as devil spirits. Lucifer's evil presence distorted the first creation of Heaven and Earth.[1] The Genesis record teaches how God has wonderfully restored the Earth we now live on. These Scriptures also include the account of His having creating Adam and Eve. They teach how God crowned them with dominion over this world.

36

However, the authority He gave to Adam and Eve threatened and diminished the plans and purposes of Lucifer. This spirit's subtle temptation, brought against Adam and Eve, resulted in the lose of their dominion over the world. Through its sly trickery Lucifer was able to steal the power and dominion of this world. Lucifer remains the god of this world today (II Corinthians 4:4). Lucifer's prideful nature led it to generate the works that are attributed to the name of Satan. It's works have earned it this loathsome title.

THE SERPENT

In E. W. Bullinger's, *The Companion Bible* he makes the following comment concerning the serpent.

> **We cannot conceive Eve as holding converse with a snake, but we can understand her being fascinated by one, apparently "an angel of light" (i.e. a glorious angel), possessing superior and supernatural knowledge.**[2]

In the same way a snake charmer charms a serpent, Lucifer beguiled Eve through its enchanting beauty. The brightness and beauty of Lucifer's appearance fascinated Eve into listening to the deceptive possibility that she could become as a god and that she would not die. Lucifer successfully enticed Eve into rebelling against the promises of her Creator. It beguiled her by its poisonous lies. It worked by its appealing, but deadly, lying deception. Eve rebelled against the Word of God. It could be that the brilliant beauty of this creature's appearance overshadowed Eve's beauty. Maybe her prideful vanity led her into the vicious trap to which she succumbed.

She failed to resist the appealing lure laid before her, "to be as gods, knowing good and evil" (Genesis 3:5b).

She partook of the bait and the consequences were extremely grave. The thrust of Lucifer's attack worked havoc upon the lives of Adam and Eve. They suffered the loss of their dominion over the earth. Their spiritual nature dried up and died. The one-flesh marriage relationship Adam and Eve had shared became distorted. They were banished from their pleasant life in the Garden of Eden and became restricted to a life of toil and labor. Their unimpeded fellowship with God vanished.

Lucifer orchestrated this vicious calamity and its far-reaching consequences.[3] Its successful attack upon Adam and Eve robbed them of their spiritual nature. The rebirth of a spiritual nature in men and women would be a long time coming to pass. As we saw earlier, it would take the fabulous ministry of our Lord Jesus Christ to bring about the miraculous rebirth of spirit life for the people of God. Recognition of how vicious and deadly the acts of Satan are should lead us to walk in the power and efficacy of the spirit God has given us, His people. The power of God in our lives equips us to withstand Satan's destructive devises. That this frontal attack upon Eve was conducted by Satan is confirmed in the book of Revelation (chapter 12:9). There it is stated plainly that the old serpent is called the devil and Satan.

SATAN

We do not need to remain ignorant of Satan's devices. The Bible record details the information we need to know about this evil spirit entity. *Young's Analytical Concordance of the Bible* defines Satan as a hater and an accuser.[4] The name Satan is the English translation of the Hebrew word meaning adversary. In one of the earliest written books of the Bible, Satan is described as "going to and fro in the earth and from walking up and down in it" (Job 1:7). The extent of this spirit's domain includes all the earth and the atmosphere surrounding it; so, Satan wonders about therein.

Revelation 12:9

And the great dragon was cast out, that old serpent, called the Devil, and Satan, which deceived the whole world: it was cast out into the earth, and its angels were cast out with it.

The next thing we're going to do is to view more details of how Satan is described biblically. Satan has never had to change its methods for one reason, they still work against the unsuspecting. Satan works by deception. Throughout history it has deceive the nations. Thankfully, the Bible gives us a record of Satan's acts. For example, we can see how Satan moved King Herod to murder the new born savior of the world. Herod failed to do so, but he did slay all the children around Bethlehem from two years old and under. Some of those possessed of Satan's spirit can be moved to the high crime of murder.

Satan is an evil influence at work (Psalms 109). In the parable Jesus told (Mark 4:15) Satan comes and takes away the Word of God that had been sowed in the hearts of those who are hearing it. This spirit seeks to nullify the Word of God by blinding the minds of those who would believe.

Jesus Christ told Simon Peter (Luke 22:31), "Satan has desired to have you, that it may sift you as wheat". Satan's desire was to destroy Peter's faith. That same evil work continues against Christian believers today. To guard against this sorted attempt we arm ourselves with the whole armor of God. (see Ephesians 6:14-18). We walk in life according to who we are in Christ Jesus. It is absolutely true that "He that is in us is greater than he (Satan) that is in the world" (I John 4:4b).

Satan is said to have power for the destruction of the flesh (I Corinthians 5:5).

This evil spirit seeks to undermine our healthy bodies. The negative, fiery, darts Satan heralds at us must not be allowed to remain in our minds. We put them down! We stay convinced that we are healed by the stripes of our Lord Jesus Christ. We lay a claim to that which belongs to us. The price has already been paid for our wholeness.

Satan himself is transformed into an angel of light (II Corinthians 11:14b).

Satan's ministers are also transformed to be the ministers of righteousness (II Corinthians 11:15). Jesus Christ warned us about the ravening wolves that are dressed in sheep's clothing. Still today, it's by their fruits that we learn who they truly are. "Even so every good tree brings forth good fruit; but a corrupt tree brings forth evil fruit" (Matthew 7:17). Remember, God has armed us with the ability to discern spirits.

Jesus commanded Satan to leave his presence. In Matthew 4:10 it reads:

Then Jesus said unto him, (it) "Get you hence Satan: for it is written, You shall worship the Lord God, and Him only shall you serve."

Jesus commanded Satan to leave his presence and it did so. By the authority of the Spirit of God, living within us, we can do the same. We don't flee from Satan, it flees from us. We have the absolute authority to send Satan away. When God teaches us about the presence of evil spirits possessing individuals we can cast them out in the name of Jesus Christ. Jesus came to destroy the works of this evil spirit, and we can continue to perform the same marvelous work.

Even though there are many other biblical records that describe Satan's nature, by this time we've seen enough to understand much of how Satan works. The natural-man of body and soul continues to be subject to this evil spirit's power. Often they even deny Satan's existence. This is not true of Christian believers who are walking by the spirit of God. The ministry and accomplishments of our Lord Jesus Christ have given Christians the ability to tread upon scorpions. Satan flees at the name of Jesus Christ upon the lips of those born-again of God's spirit.

Ephesians 6:12-13

For we wrestle not against flesh and blood, but against principalities, against powers, against the rulers of the darkness of this world, against spiritual wickedness in high places. Wherefore take unto you the whole armor of God, that you may be able to withstand in the evil day, and having done all, to stand.

THE ADVERSARY

The Bible declares the evil fallen angel spirit we are discussing, to be an adversary. The meaning of adversary has many different senses throughout Scripture. Some of these senses include; an enemy, to distress, to straighten, to bind, an accuser, an opponent, and to be in opposition. Job declared of his adversarial spirit, "Oh, that mine adversary had written a book" (Job 31:35b). The adversary of God's people remains clothed in secrecy. Its secrecy keeps it shrouded from five senses' perception. Those who are savvy about spiritual matters are able to understand the cause behind the working of this evil opponent. Job certainly knew the cause behind his troubles was, indeed, works of his adversary. Still today, this adversarial spirit has not written a book to describe its methods and its works. However, a few Scripture references will teach us some of what we need to know about this opponent.

The Apostle Paul's message to the Thessalonian Church was, "we would have come unto you, even I Paul, once and again; but Satan (his adversary) hindered us (I Thessalonians 2:18). The messenger of Satan (an adversarial spirit) was sent to buffet the Apostle Paul (II Corinthian11:15). Paul's work was to spread the Gospel of the Lord Jesus Christ. Paul's purposes were contrary to the purposes of Satan. Satan's activities were designed to destroy the Word of the Lord. This is why Satan became an adversarial spirit to the wonderful, giving, purposes of the great Apostle Paul. Satan will remain an adversarial spirit to Christian believers until it is consumed in the "lake of fire" prepared for it and its devil spirits.

The Apostle Peter asked fellow believers to be vigilant and watchful concerning their adversary.

I Peter 5:8-9

Be sober, be vigilant; because your adversary the devil, as a roaring lion, walks about, seeking whom he may devour: Whom resist stedfast in the faith, knowing that the same afflictions are accomplished in your brethren that are in the world.

First and foremost, this adversarial spirit is an opponent to God and therefore is an opponent to the people of God. Its aim remains to defeat God Almighty. As the accuser of God's people it seeks to cast condemnations upon them. Keeping them in sin consciousness is its goal. By hindering God's people, it hinders the plan of redemption initiated by our Creator. The renewed-mind believing of Christians enables them to lay their claim to the perfect Word of God. They reject the adversary's lying suggestions that are to the contrary.

Romans 8:1

There is therefore now no condemnation to them which are in Christ Jesus, who walk not after the flesh, but after the Spirit.

Romans 8:33-35

Who shall lay any thing to the charge of God's elect? It is God that justifies.

Who is he that condemns? It is Christ that died, yea rather, that is risen again, who is even at the right hand of God, who also makes intercession for us. Who shall separate us from the love of Christ? Shall tribulation, or distress, or persecution, or famine, or nakedness, or peril, or sword?

The adversary is not limited to vicious frontal attacks. It baits and suckers those whose hearts are fixed upon the treasures of this world. As a trickster, it dangles "sweet cherries" before the eyes of those not aware of its evil intentions. Just like it promised the Lord Jesus Christ all the kingdoms of the world, it promises the unsuspecting the riches of this world and all the pleasures they can enjoy. The way to defeat this adversary is to keep one's mind and heart fixed upon heavenly rewards and everlasting pleasures.

I John 2:15-17

Love not the world, neither the things that are in the world. If any man love the world, the love of the Father is not in him. For all that is in the world, the lust of the flesh, and the lust of the eyes, and the pride of life, is not of the Father but is of the world. And the world passes away, and the lust thereof: but he that does the will of God abides for ever.

The adversary will continue its efforts to undermine the health and well-being of God's people. Saints and sinners alike are sometimes plagued with health issues. If health becomes an issue with Christian believers they have a sound remedy; their healing is available. They can face health issues by confessing and claiming the miraculous healing God has provided for His sons and daughters. The suffering and stripes of the Lord Jesus Christ paid the price for their healing and wholeness.

I Peter 2:24

Who his own self bare our sins in his own body on the tree, that we, being dead to sins, should live unto righteousness: by whose stripes you were healed.

Healing and wholeness are God's gifts to every Christian Believer. They need to stand against the adversary's attempt to steal and destroy their health and wholeness. The fireballs of their adversary may come at them blazing. They may be confronted with negative pronouncements like some of the following:

"The doctor said I have liver cancer and it can't be treated. He said I might have only six months to live."

"I have had a spinal operation and it has not relieved my excruciating pain. What am I going to do?"

"I have caught the COVID virus and I think it's going to do me in!"

It's truly a big-time mistake to allow such fireballs to lodge in the mind. When one confesses them to be true, that which they are confessing is going to come to pass. What they believe in their heart is then working against them. The need is to cast off what the adversary is saying about them and begin to confess and believe what God has to say about them. Just whom are they going to believe? Will they believe the adversary who is seeking to take their life or a loving God who is seeking to give them a healthy, robust, life?

Don't give way to the adversary. The God and Father of our Lord Jesus Christ is the Creator and Giver of Life. His will is that His people prosper, and be in health.[5] He is not the author of sickness, disease, or death. When His people are alive and prospering and in good health, they can praise God! They can love and thank Him for the blessings He has bestowed upon them. They are absolutely of no good to God dead! God wants them living and loving and praising Him for all His wonderful works.

THE DEVIL

Jesus Christ, in his parable of the sower, called the devil, "the wicked one" (Matthew 13:19). Some of the other names for the devil are tempter, Beelzebub, destroyer, oppressor, murderer, Belial, and Father of Lies. There are still other names. A list of over 30 of the devil's names can be compiled from Scripture references. By this time we are qualified to identify the devil's characteristics and how it works its purposes to kill, steal, and destroy (John 10:10). The devil works behind the scenes to accomplish its aims. The secrecy of its moves is designed to defeat the promises of God's Word. As a spirit being, it marshals its powers to intervene and interrupt the order and harmony of God's creation. The devil is the cause behind disastrous storms and catastrophes. It is the cause behind massive confusion. It is the force that works destruction and death. But, the devil is a limited spirit being whose evil workings our Lord Jesus Christ exposed. We are no longer subjected to this evil spirit's devices nor should we ever fear its power.

One day, in the future, the devil will receive its eternal judgment. God will cast this adversarial spirit, called the devil, into a lake of fire and brimstone. The prophet Ezekiel relayed God's Word about the devil's final destination.

Ezekiel 26:21

I will make you a terror, and you shall be no more: though you be sought for, yet shall you never be found again, saith the Lord God.

Yes, that day is still in the future, and what a glorious day that will be! The reality for now, however, is that the devil remains at work; it's still alive and kicking. One of its prominent works in history, and also in our day and time, is the construction and distribution of its devilish doctrines. Doctrines are normally thought of as hard and fast truths. They are thought to be trustworthy beliefs; you may rely upon what they seek to teach. However, practically speaking, though embraced as truth, they may contain errors and even outright lies. This can certainly be said of some religious doctrines. Beyond a shadow of a doubt, this can be said of devilish doctrines. These doctrines are a cleverly devised mixture of truth and lies.

> **I Timothy 4:1-2**
>
> **Now the Spirit speaks expressly, that in the latter times some shall depart from the faith, giving heed to seducing spirits, and doctrines of devils; Speaking lies in hypocrisy; having their conscience seared with a hot iron.**

Doctrines are developed upon a system of beliefs. However, devilish doctrines are founded upon falsehood and lies; but they are presented as truth. They are a counterfeit of truth. The counterfeit has to be close to the original; close enough to fool the observer. There may be some truth in a devilish doctrine but truth cannot be predicated or substantiated by lies.

Devilish reasoning can enter the human mind through distorted, evil, thinking. The individual may not be aware that they have accepted devilish lies because they have been blinded to the truth. Please remember that if the devil's fiery darts are allowed to lodge in the mind, the heart may one day embrace them. Unrealistic thinking and selfish desires, can become a seedbed for devilish doctrines to take root. Confusion, fear, egotism, lust, and pride are "bad seeds" that invite devilish doctrines to sprout and grow.

The devil wheels a great influence throughout our society. It maintains a relentless impact on our citizenry. The end result of this is greater corruption in the world, and less and less of any true justice. Today, television and social media provide the kind of brainwashing repetition that drives lies and falsehoods into the vulnerable human mind. With enough promotion and repetition, these lying precepts can be mistakenly accepted to be true. It is sad to say, but when individuals finally believe and embrace a lie their consciousness of truth becomes seared, as with a hot iron. When individuals become fully persuaded about falsehoods they become overshadowed by a false reality. They are on a sinking sand foundation because they have actually rejected truth.

Some of our younger generation have been schooled to embrace numbers of lying falsehoods. They are displaying a Marx's mentality. They have carried what they embraced with them into the positions they occupy in business and government. Consequently, much of our political leadership's decision-making is predicated upon falsehoods. They have fallen into the trap set by the devil. For example, our government has fully embraced the climate change hoax.

It is so obvious, perilous times have come. The prominence of evil is worldwide. Corrupt governments are failing their people. Political processes here in the United States are undermining the freedoms our citizenry have enjoyed for generations. Communistic government continues to maintain brutal control over the people of China and Russia, and dictatorships control many of the smaller nations. The misery of the Ukrainian War has been televised before us constantly. The recent COVID pandemic has destroyed the lives of millions. Thousands here in the United States are dying from illegal drugs .The news media is quick to inform the public of horrific evils that are occurring day-by-day around the world. Their depressing news is a downer. They fill our ears and our vision with the evil works of the devil. We might be better off to shut the media completely out of our hearing; just turn them off and let them stew in their own juices.

Surely you have noticed, the devil remains the god of this world. It seeks to destroy our health, our happiness, and our well being. It is the source bringing about the decay and destruction of the fundamental systems the people of this land have enjoyed in the past. However, there is no need for God's people to become discouraged by the multiplication of evil. The power and presence of our Heavenly Father resides within us. He that lives within us is far greater than who marshals evil in this world.

The return of our Lord Jesus Christ will deliver us (his own) from this present evil world. Those of us who are born-again of God's spirit will be raised up to meet our Lord in the air, and so shall we ever be with Him. Those who remain on Earth, after the gathering together of God's people, are in for perilous times. The choices by which they will be confronted are horrific; they are in for very dark days. They will have to turn to God to be delivered.

After a set time, known only to God Almighty, the Lord Jesus Christ will again come to Earth, along with his resurrected saints. Then he will establish order, justice, and peace; evil will be removed from this world. The established order of Christ's millennial reign will bring an end to the works of the devil. No longer will the works of this evil spirit undermine the children of God. Until that day comes, God's people need to maintain their heavenly view whereby they are seated with Christ on the right hand of God. The Bible record has said it with inspiring words:

Ephesians 2:6

And (God) has raised us up together, and made us sit together in heavenly places in Christ Jesus.

The power and presence of God's spirit within us brings victory after victory over the devil. Even in this present evil world we rejoice that our names are written in the Book of Life. We are no longer subject to the evil works of darkness. We have nothing to fear. Truly, we are in command.

In the next chapter we are going to examine the first of the five devilish doctrines discussed by this author. So, hold on tight, here we go. The road we must travel may get a little bumpy at times. Nonetheless, when we arrive at our destination we will have exposed devilish lies and made room for the reality of truth to become the foundation of our thinking and the morality of our consciousness. By this time we are able to properly access and judge devilish doctrines. We can view them from the enlightening stance of spiritual discernment. Let's get started!

1 See Genesis 1:1-2

2 Bullinger, E. W. *The Companion Bible,* Appendix 19 The Serpent of Genesis 3, p.24-25, Zondervan , Grand Rapids, MI 1974

3 See Genesis 3:13-19

4 Young, Robert, *Young's Analytical Concordance of the Bible,* p. 836 (Satan), Eerdmans, Grand Rapids, MI, 1971

5 See III John verse 2

CHAPTER 4

POSSESSION OR CHOICE

To whom do you belong? The Bible teaches that those of us born of God's spirit are not our own; rather we've been bought with a price.

I Corinthians 6:19-20

What? Know you not that your body is the Temple of the Holy Spirit which is in you, which you have of God, and you are not your own? For you are bought with a price: therefore, glorify God in your body, and in your spirit, which are God's.

God owns us, but He does not control us! His love for us has endowed us with freedom of will. We can live our lives by choice. Our inherent ability of choice is a gift; it belongs to us. God truly expects that we will honor Him with what we choose to do, or not to do. God's goodness has rained down upon His people. His desire is that we respond in kind; that we seek to please Him in all things. His high calling is that we will, by our freedom of choice, seek to love Him with all our mind, heart and strength. Surely this is a bare minimum expectation. Surely this is a reasonable response for His gracious love and His mercy upon our lives; even when we blunder in our sins. Surely this is the right response to His giving us freedom of life to choose, and also the promise to live with Him eternally in His glorious kingdom.

We need to guard our free will standing by making responsible choices. That requires guarding our hearts so that we are never waylaid by devilish attempts to cast us down. Possessing the human mind is a common tool utilized by the devil. Devil spirits can, and will, direct the possessed individual to accomplish their evil purposes. The devil possessed individual has relinquished his or her freedom of will; they are no longer in control of their behavior. The evil spirit manipulates them. Devil spirit attacks are grounded and fostered in secrecy. Their tempting suggestions are appealing, but their dark, shady, methods are entrapments. They promise inviting pleasures, treasures, riches, and even exceeding glory. However, the devil's lying words are like a dangerously, explosive mine, cleverly hidden beneath the ground. When the unsuspecting step on them they suffer grave injury, dismemberment, and even death. Their words are purposely designed to steal precious words of truth. Their words are suitably designed to trick people into changing their thinking. Heeding the devil's words will blind one's ability to shun the evil and choose the godly.

Words are vital to our understanding. They provide the mental images that enable us to communicate with others. Words that appeal to our feelings, likes and dislikes, fears, joys and pleasures, among others, motivate us to form our conclusions. Positive, truthful, words can steer us into that which is right and pleasing to our Heavenly Father. Devilish words will steer us into the dark waters of rebellion against the God and Father of our Lord Jesus Christ.

Matthew 12:34b-37

For out of the abundance of the heart the mouth speaks. A good man out of the good treasure of the heart brings forth good things: and an evil man out of the evil treasure brings forth evil things. But I (Jesus) say unto you, That every idle word that men shall speak, they shall give account thereof in the day of judgment. For by your words you shall be justified, and by your words you shall be condemned.

It's easy for words and phrases that have underlying meanings to creep into our vocabularies. Some of these words are derived from pagan idolatry. Consequently, they subtlety promote devilish lies that are designed to rob us of truth. They lead us away from acknowledging that which is truthful, wholesome, and godly. They lead us away from truth by exalting falsehoods. They appear to have legitimate meanings but the opposite is true. Destiny, predestination, fate, luck, and chance are words (concepts) that fit into this category. We need to use due caution when speaking them. Words like these have meanings that are referred to in philosophy as deterministic doctrines.

Webster's definition of determinism is as follows; "the doctrine that one's choice of action is not free but is determined by a sequence of causes independent of his will. ssentially, this doctrine describes supposed forces that undermine our freedom of choice. All of these words, and their concepts, have become a playground in which devil spirits work their devises. As we work through this chapter the reader can see how these devilish concepts have been firmly established in our culture. We are going to individually treat each of these suspicious words and show how the devil seeks to implant these ideas into our vocabulary and finally into our believing.

DESTINY

Some people believe a force called "destiny" controls human life. Do you have an inevitable destiny controlling you? What we really have in the development of destiny's meaning is the emergence of a lying claim. Clearly, ancient gods were powerless, but the idolaters who bowed down to them said, "They have power." Consequently, they believed in a lying proclamation. They falsely claimed the powers of the gods they worship were great enough to determine what was going to occur in their lives. This is the sense of the meaning of the Latin word "destinare." Destiny's meaning took root in the concept of a false god's ability to determine a given outcome in a person's life; to set their boundaries and to determine how their life ends up.

Destiny has become a "trickster" word. Its modern-day meaning shadows and conceals the force responsible for determining an outcome. The description of whom or what that is responsible for the action in this word remains unnamed and even masked by obscurity. The unnamed force operating in the concept of destiny is left to the surmising of the individual hearing this word. It is the masked, obscured force in the modern meaning of destiny that makes room for the devil to operate its intentions. When the implied power in the meaning of destiny is fully named then we can grasp its deviant, idolatrous, meaning.

Destiny has no power. It cannot proclaim its own works. Someone must stand up on its behalf and voice its lying claims. In reality, destiny is nothing more than a lofty personification of attractive, but worthless, words. Its appealing ideas are designed to hook and snare the innocent. Here are a few of the enticing lies the devil promotes through the idea of destiny:

- Destiny shows favoritism. It rewards individuals even though they have done nothing to receive its favor.

- Destiny pays no attention to morality; it elevates both the good and the bad.

- Destiny calls for greatness. It chooses individuals for great purposes.

- Destiny calls; it calls individuals but it also calls nations.

- Destiny is an attractive force maneuvering minute human affairs and circumstances; it acts unexpectedly.

- Destiny cannot be summoned nor can it be appeased. It determines what is meant to be.

- Destiny dashes into pieces the best efforts and high ambitions of men.

Satan utilizes the concept of destiny to deceive. By words of intrigue, people are entrapped. By the constant use of this idolatrous concept, people become attracted to its familiar idea. The dazzle and appeal of romanticized, whimsical, words dupe people into believing outlandish lies. The fundamental lie embraced within the concept of destiny is that the individual's efforts, energy, and discipline are not the controlling power in life. Supposedly the highest controlling power remains that unseen-force out there. It is the ultimate cause bringing a blessing or a cursing - it's destiny! Lies, lies, and more lies; but we know better! We must remain in control of our own facilities. We posses the God-given power of choice.

PREDESTINATION

The Bible does use the word predestinate. As we shall see, the biblical usage of predestinate is vastly different from the pagan concept.[2] Any valid discussion about predestinate must take into consideration the predestinator. The following Scripture uses the word predestinate.

Ephesians 1:4-5

According as He (God) has chosen us in Him before the foundation of the world, that we should be holy and without blame before Him in love: Having predestinated us unto the adoption (sonship) of children by Jesus Christ to Himself, according to the good pleasure of His will.

Because God is all knowing, His view of eternity precedes the beginning and the end. His foreknowledge precedes our choices. He does not determine our choices; however, He knows, in advance, what we will choose. The outstanding problem people have with the word "predestinate" comes from mistakenly associating it with the concept of destiny. Within the concept of destiny a supposed god, or some unknown force, always does the choosing, and then casts its decision upon human life. The word "predestinate", is used four times in the Bible and it never refers to God's determining anything apart from our ability to choose. God will never cast anything upon us that would negate our ability to choose. God knows the future. He knew ahead of time the choices we would make in our lives. He knew that we would believe in the resurrection of Jesus Christ from the dead. God knew we would decide to make Jesus Christ the lord of our lives. God knew we would react to His Word in just this manner, that we would become sons of God, born of His spirit.

FATE

Mythical references to the supposed powers of pagan gods and goddesses formed the foundation upon which the idea of fate rested through centuries of history. Fate is often referred to as a power of determination.[3] This supposed power exists somewhere in the heavens but hovers beyond our sight. It is said to possess the uncanny ability to act upon us by overstepping our ability to determine our personal future. This, supposed, great power of determination cancels out our freedom of will and we have no choice, we must submit to it. According to its popular concept fate's power literally takes away our freedom to act. The idea of fate stands in opposition to freedom. All of these weird ideas are precepts associated with fate.

Sadly, far too many have bought into the phony, groundless, logic about fate. You and I constantly hear misguided references to what has been caused by this counterfeit power. Phrases like "as fate would have it", or "a twist of fate", are commonplace. Often people are driven by the belief that fate has called them to success, and even greatness. Others consider themselves to be paralyzed by what fate has adversely decreed. We constantly hear the fatalistic excuses of individuals that embrace this kind of logic. They are too quick to abandon their responsibilities and lay the blame for their failure at fate's door.

When it comes to determining reality beyond the five senses, worldly-minded people often turn to ridiculous, weird, explanations, including the concept of fate. Understanding dynamic causes that are beyond the capacity of our five senses requires spiritual perception and awareness. Men and women who are born of God's spirit have the ability to discern spiritual matters.

To comprehend the spiritual significance behind fate's development, and why the concept remains active today, it is essential to recognize the devil's handiwork.

Maybe you have never associated devil spirit possession with the idea of fate; however, they are very much connected. When men abandoned the glory of the incorruptible God and sought to glorify the gods they had made, the devil gained an opening through which it could work its purposes. The idolatrous gods of antiquity were completely without power. They were not capable of possessing or controlling anyone or anything. In contrast to man-made gods, devil

59

spirits can and do possess human individuals who yield to their control.

The Christian believer should have no problem recognizing the doctrines that surround fate. We are not going to be carried away by "every wind of doctrine." We are not going to be taken in and deceived by false theologies. To do so will rob us of both our power and our peace. False theologies are always floating around and they are designed to blind and deceive. However, to walk in fellowship with God brings great joy, peace, and power. By manifesting the power and love of God that resides within us we can walk victoriously over the "wiles of the devil" and any lying doctrine that seeks to verify the meaning of fate.

LUCK'S DOCTRINE

The fundamental claim about luck is its power.[4] Many people believe in luck's power to bestow blessings; that it can supply needs and wants. They also believe the power of bad luck can bring harm to their lives . All these claims add up to something of great importance if they are factual. If the assertions made about luck are true, then we have an exalted "god force" operating in and about us. This supposed force is not the God and Father of our Lord Jesus Christ. This obscured wayward luck doctrine is exactly what the proponents of luck are setting forth. They believe this "god-force" called luck is alive and operating in the universe today. Throughout most of history, there have been those that have stood up and proclaimed luck's reality. They say it is real; that it exists, and it operates either for them

60

or against them. Our generation is no different, people today are still confessing the same bogus beliefs about luck. They continue to believe in the validity of luck's power. Just how did this faulty reasoning get into their thinking?

By tracing the origin of the word "fortune" we will be able to see how the word "luck" gained such a prominent place in the vocabulary of modern-day Americans. Our word fortune developed from beliefs about the Roman goddess, Fortuna. She was worshipped primarily for benefits but her gifts were rewarded according to her whims and discretion. The focal point of her appeal centered upon what the Romans believed was her power to deliver a benefit. There were many gods and goddesses that were believed to "dole out" doom, but not Fortuna. She was not feared, rather she was sought after for her blessings. To seek the acclaimed favor of this goddess was believed to be a legitimate means of achieving success.

The most fundamental idea about luck matches the theological meaning of fortune. The heart of fortune's meaning remains " the ability to bestow prosperity." The Romans attributed "the bestowing of prosperity" to Fortuna.

Their misguided belief about the ability of Fortuna to bestow prosperity has stayed intact and travels to us by two linguistic paths. One pathway was through France. The old French word "fortune" emphasized unpredictability. The other linguistic path was through the Germanic and Scandinavian languages. The early low German word "luk" is closely related to the modern Dutch "geluk." The prefix "ge" is employed in the Middle High German, "gelucke." This is the source of the modern German that means good fortune. The English dropped the prefix "g" and translated German into what is now our word "luck." Still, to this very day, the English word luck conveys the ancient idea of the bestowing of prosperity by the power of a god.

The design of luck theology is devilishly crafted to refute the abiding reality of God and the sure promises of His Word. Demented teachings about the "luck god" are, in effect, designed to rob our Heavenly Father of the praise and honor He is due. The lying doctrines surrounding the idea of luck claim that it is the source of prosperity and protection. For example, when an unexpected blessing comes, the supposed power of luck is credited. To confess that luck bestowed a benefit is to deny God's handiwork. It is to deny His love and that the benefits are from Him alone. It is to turn one's back on God and give the praise that belongs to Him to a false metaphysical devilish entity. To embrace luck is to believe in a doctrine devised by devilish influence and intent.

Luck is not an inexplicable force that cannot be understood, explained, or accounted for. Neither is it a source of prosperity; nor is it the cause of evil and destruction; that, in fact, is the workmanship of the devil. The following is a three-sentence concise nutshell summation for the meaning of luck: luck is a religious devotion; an idolatrous confession. It's a corruption of sound thought and will. It is a misguided belief in the existence of a metaphysical god. Luck is a denial of cause and effect. A confession of luck is passive submission to fatalistic thinking. Luck is a doctrine of devils that stand diametrically opposed to the Word of God. This may not be the dictionary definition but it is free from cloudiness. This definition accurately points out truth and exposes errors.

CHANCES ARE?

Sound judgment has produced a body of information that refutes the concept of chance.[5] Throughout history, there have been those who stood in opposition to the whimsical uncertainty of chance philosophy. Modern deterministic philosophy accepts that nothing occurs by chance.

> No matter what happens, there is always a reason why that happened rather than something else. This is called the principle of sufficient reason. Determinism asserts that for whatever happens there is always a cause, or that nothing happens by chance.[6]

Science is generally concerned with theories about cause and effect; but, it has little or nothing to say about PURPOSE. However, both cause and purpose are intrinsically built into the operation and structure of the universe, and life itself. Without purpose and cause everything would fall apart and go drifting away. Nothing would stay intact and nothing could keep its identity. Set bounds and limits of activity make life what it is. Set purposes and causes are the sustaining building blocks that makes our live work the way it does. The following verses tell about God's creation of all things in heaven and on earth, but it also teaches that it is His purpose and design that holds it all together.

Colossians 1:16,17

For by Him were all things created, that are in heaven, and that are in earth, visible and invisible, whether they be thrones, or dominions, or principalities, or powers: all things were created by Him, and for Him:and He is before all things, and by Him all things consist (cohere, or hold together).

We, humans, will always need to answer to a higher power, because man has never created anything. We are not capable of creation in the biblical sense. We are the creation, and we must ultimately answer to the purposes and causes our Creator has designed. Both the broad and specific perimeters of life are God's design.

Romans 9:20

No, but O man, who are you that replies against God? Shall the thing formed say to Him that formed it, Why have you made me thus?

The design of our Creator does not include the operation of chance; not even on a microscopic level. Thus, there is no right response to chance, for chance does not exist. Chance does not fit within the context of purpose. God has built order and harmony throughout the universe. A sheep behaves like a sheep. A duck behaves like a duck. They were created to behave in a precise manner. Our massive planet Earth continues to revolve around the Sun with just enough tilting back and forth to make our changing seasons an unchanging certainty.

God built order and harmony into the very fabric of life. We can count on the constant order and processes that make life work. Sunshine and rain, seedtime and harvest, are a sure constant; and gravity is always there. The air we breathe is there, praise God! Water to satisfy our thirst is always there. What are the chances of all this changing? Anyone can see the concept of chance just does not fit into biological and physical spheres of order and harmony. Nor does chance fit into the functioning of spiritual realities. What a wonderful creation God has made and none of this order is subject to chance. To repeat a Bible verse again:

Genesis 8: 22

While the earth remains, seed-time and harvest, and cold and heat, and summer and winter, and day and night shall not cease.

There are exceptions to order and harmony in the Universe. The exception to order is disorder. But, these exceptions could be better described as interruptions. Order and harmony normally exist throughout the Universe. The ocean stays put within its set boundaries unless an outside force interrupts those boundaries. Interruptions such as title waves, volcano eruptions, tornadoes, earthquakes, and hurricanes change order to disorder. A healthy body is normal; however, disorder changes wholeness into sickness and disease. Often we hear these events ascribed to chance, but just as often they are described as "acts of God." Both opinions are wrong. As it has been stated previously "chance is the cause of nothing" and God is not the author of confusion.

God is not the initiator of death, disorder, and destruction. He does not cause catastrophe; but, the god of this world does. The god of this world is the devil and it remains the archenemy of God. The devil is not only a thief but continues to be the source of evil, death, disorder, and destruction. The devil works behind the scenes to accomplish its aims. As a spirit being it marshals its powers to interrupt the order and harmony of God's creation. The devil is the operating cause behind disastrous storms and catastrophes. It is the cause behind massive confusion; and, it is the force that works destruction and death. The devilish doctrine of chance is that life is subject to unknown powers operating upon us and about us; powers that can promote us, but are also able to destroy our lives. However, the devil is a limited spirit being whose evil workings have been exposed by our Lord, Jesus Christ. We are no longer subject to its devices nor should we ever fear its power.

I John 4:4

You are of God, little children, and have overcome them: because greater is He that is in you, than it (the devil and its people) that is in the world.

Some do not believe spiritual realities exist. Therefore, they mistakenly attribute the works of the devil, to the preposterous, supposed entity they call chance. They mistakenly believe chance to be the cause behind massive disasters and destructive events. They attribute chance to less spectacular events as well. The natural-minded individual who does not believe God exists and who does not believe the devil exists, can and does say chance exists. Anemic confessions of chance are often the product of a lazy and doubting mind. Those who reject God might believe anything.

God's design for life and living leaves nothing to chance. What God has built into the fabric of life is choice. We, humans, are free and rational beings, well we are rational most of the time. Nevertheless, we have the power of choice built into our capacity. We can be made to do little that is against our will. We can choose to love God and believe His Word; this is always profitable. We can also choose to deny God and His Word; this is never profitable. In the end, we choose that which we think, and we also choose what to embrace with our believing actions. It is God who has designed us with this tremendous ability. Having designed us with this capability gives us the privilege of choosing to love Him.

The first thing that happened was God chose us. God chose us before the foundation of the world; and, we have the personal freedom to respond. We can choose to love God; we can choose to serve Him and to be thankful to Him day-by-day. God made us in such a way that we could have great fellowship with him. We can respond to His love for us and God responds to our love and faithfulness to Him. Choice always means responsibility. It is our responsibility and privilege to choose God; to love God, and to believe His Matchless Word. The concept of chance seeks to exclude the operation of God living in our daily lives. It is, however, by His power that we live and move and have our being. We can cast the thoughts of our hearts upon Him; there our hearts will be safe. We can cast our cares upon Him for He cares for us.

Here is a great truth all of us need to understand. God is not the author of deterministic doctrines. Just no category in life is outside of God's care, God's power, and God's love. No matter how big the need you may have, God is big enough to take care of you. No matter how big your failure and sin, God is big enough to cleanse you. No matter how incurable the disease God is big enough to heal you. No matter how heavy your heart's burden, God's comfort is big enough to make it light. If life looks hopeless to you, God is still big enough. He is the God of promise and Hope. He is God Almighty! So what do you need in your life? God is always big enough. God has left nothing to chance!

1 *Webster's New World Dictionary*, World Pub., N.Y., 1968, s.v. "determinism"

2 Ibid., s.v. "predestination"

3 Ibid., s.v."fate"

4 Ayto, John, *Arcade Dictionary of Word Origins*, Arcade Pub., N.Y., 1968, s.v. "luck"

5 *Webster's New World Dictionary*, World Pub., N.Y., 1968, s.v. "luck"

6 Encyclopedia American, Americana Corp., N.Y., 1962, s.v. "determinism"

CHAPTER 5

TRANSGENDER LIES

It is a lying devilish doctrine that an individual can change their gender from a man to a woman or a woman to a man. Nonetheless, the infestation of devilish lies has infected the gullible minds of individuals seeking to change their sex. The devil is actively working to make sex change an accepted practice. Lies about its normality, and its acceptance by society, are truly evil, devilish, ploys.

Just what is the attitude one should have toward those who are participating in a supposed gender change? We want to be kind, loving and understanding even sympathetic, and tolerant among those with whom we live and work. To do so is certainly a good practice; however, it is not a good practice to walk silently by those who are opposing themselves and flirting with the destruction of their lives!

The Christian believer's work is that of reconciling men and women to God our Heavenly Father. When individuals, who have opposed themselves, begin to search for deliverance, God's people can minister to their needs. They can provide the healing and deliverance

69

sought for. So, this is the work Christian believers are to do. Their work is not to belittle or to judge or to cast condemnation upon those they meet in the daily intercourse of life. On the contrary, the Christian believer's work is to speak loving words of truth and hope, and encouragement to those who need healing and deliverance. This is exactly what the words in this chapter seek to do.

Those choosing to have a sex operation are opposing themselves.[1]They are casting away their God-given endowment and slipping into the entrapment of a slippery slope. The strangely, queered, motivations of those who are traveling this pathway need to be brought to light. That they have a gender identity problem is their patsy terminology for a selfish, twisted, ungodly desire. Their vain calm is, "I can't help it." Before deliverance can come to them the true cause of their problem needs to be confronted! For many of them, the problem by which they are overwhelmed is devil spirit possession.

Our Heavenly Father designed the human mind to have the ability to choose. Individuals can choose to travel the road of godly, upright, morality. They can also choose to travel the dark road of evil. Traveling the dark road of evil can open individuals up to demonic influence. A devil spirit can gain control by alluring and persuading an individual to accept its presence, its nature, and its works. When an individual allows the cunning entrapments of a devil spirit to take root in their life devil spirit possession may occur. The devil spirit possessed man or woman has relinquished their ability to choose. When this occurs the possessing spirit exercises and manipulates the mental processes of the individual. Such an individual is literally possessed. They are under the power and control of a devil spirit.

God has endowed His People with the ability to free the devil possessed. They can bring deliverance to those individuals seeking to regain their freedom from possession. Devil spirits will flee when they are commanded to do so in the name of Jesus Christ. This is the outstanding method that will bring about deliverance to those possessed of the devil.

Next, we are going to view how various groups of individuals voice their opinions and beliefs about the practice of gender change.

GOD'S VIEW

Gender change is, first off, a denial of what God created an individual to be. It is acting like God has made a mistake. The normality of God's handiwork in creating the bodies of men and women the way they are is blatantly obvious. Men are designed to be men and man's counterpart is the woman.

Genesis 1:27b

Male and female created He (God) them.

God did not intend that a man or a woman should attempt to change their given design. As a matter of fact, it is absolutely impossible for them to do so! Sex change is against the established order of God's design. He has never made a gender mix-up mistake. It is the misdirected attempts of men and women who are seeking to change their God-given bodies; that is the mistake.

Nowhere in nature has there ever been the alteration of one species that then develops into another kind of species. Nor has nature ever produced a sex change in the human species. The arbitrary efforts on the part of a few individuals to change a man into a woman, or a woman into a man, are dismal failures. Sowing a penis into where a vagina belongs does not turn a woman into a man. She remains a woman who now has a penis sown into her body. The same is true of a man seeking to be a woman. Removing his penis and medically constructing a vagina opening into him does not make him a woman. He remains a man without a penis.

Those who are seeking such a change still have the same body parts. Their liver has not changed. Their kidneys have not changed. Their hearts have not changed. Their hearts pump the same blood and their other body parts are still intact. They have not changed internally. Their efforts to become someone else have utterly failed. A woman who seeks to become a man cannot produce sperm; that truly is impossible. A sex change on the part of a man does not give him the ability to birth a child. The inner organs of a man cannot, and will never, develop a child. God knew exactly what He was doing when He created a man to be a man and a woman to be a woman. Any attempt to alter His fixed design is certainly not according to His plan and purpose. It is contrary to His perfect construction of the human body.

UNSAVORY MEDICAL PRACTICES

The first gender change surgery was performed on a female in the early 1960's. The location was in the Netherlands, in the city of

Arnhem. The Dutch plastic surgeon who performed the operation was Dr. Woudstra.[2] A strong protest was voiced against the procedure. Even the Dutch Parliament investigated the matter. Sadly, however, by the 1970's the gender change procedure was fully accepted in the Netherlands.

The first gender change operation in the United States was performed at Johns Hopkins University.[3] They launched their gender change procedure in 1966. After ten years of research, they concluded that those who received sex change surgery had not changed their lives for the better. Despite their conclusion, gender change procedures are still being performed by plastic surgeons today. Gender change procedures have consequently left a trail of misery upon those who have undergone the operation.[4]

Have you ever met a doctor who came across to you with god-like authority, puffed up, and flaunting his or her knowledge? Doctors who fall into this category sometimes do as much harm as good. When you begin to weigh the misery and suffering of those who have undergone transgender operations against the benefits they can enjoy, misery and suffering exceeds the benefit drastically. Truly, it just is not worth it. It's a loser for those who have undergone the procedure. [5]

So, the obvious question that comes to mind is why would a reputable doctor perform an operation of this nature? If his or her motive is compassion it's misguided; if it is greed then shame on them. Have they fallen into an "everybody else is doing it " mentality? Those who are choosing to perform this procedure are harming the individuals they claim to be helping. Is it that their pompous out of bound egos are leading them to continue this type of surgery? Have they failed to recognize the delusion of the weak-minded individuals who are seeking for them to change their sex?

The procedures required in sex change operations are extensive. For example, a man seeking to look like a woman may desire to do away with his beard growth. The procedure requires removing each hair follicle by inserting a shock needle into the cell structure of the follicle. Electrical current is delivered through the needle and the cell structure of the follicle is destroyed. There are around 1,270 individual beard follicles on the face of a man. The procedure to remove all of those follicles requires treatments lasting twelve to eighteen months. The cost for each treatment is in the category of 200 plus dollars. The unseemly treatment is both painful and costly. This is just a modest example of the costly, painful, and horrific experiences transgenders endure. According to Inside Business News, even patients with insurance benefits still face large bills in the six-figure category.[6]

The medical personnel who are accommodating the delusions, and sorted desires, of their patients, need to stop what they are practicing upon these people. They need to refuse to accommodate the deranged, misguided desires of the individuals who have chosen to butcher their God-given endowment. Surely it's not too late for the medical profession to reevaluate this highly questionable medical procedure. The moral and spiritual aspects of what they have been practicing need to come to the foreground of their thinking and decision-making. Those doctors who are Christian believers need to discern if devil spirit possession is the driving force influencing an individual to undergo a sex change. Numerous states have banned the procedure in youth all together.[7]

Those performing these operations are not innocent bystanders, but rather they are contributing to an outrageous distortion of the human body. They need to lay aside this surgical practice and stop its use altogether. The troubling desires of the people who are asking to change into a different sex are asking for something that cannot come to pass. No amount of surgery, steroid, and hormonal treatments can facilitate the change they are seeking. Their desires are based upon a total disregard for the wonderful womanhood or manhood DNA nature they received from their parents. They certainly need to consider that their actions infer that God has mistakenly given them the wrong sex. The lying, devilish, doctrine that a woman can be changed into a man or a man can be changed into a woman, has lodged in their thinking. The acceptance of this lying doctrine will bring misery, defeat, and ultimately destruction. A high percentage of the so-call transgenders end up seeking suicide to relieve their misery.[8] This is especially true of the seriously abused children who have undergone this devilish operation. According to a 2015 study, one out of three of these ill-treated children died of suicide.

TRANSGENDER REGRETS

Sex change is basically a one-way street. It can't be changed back with the expectation of returning to the way one was originally.[9] Undergoing the operation means enduring the pain of surgery and the endurance of a long recovery; that's if things are going well. Those who have undergone a sex operation should not expect acceptance from the communities in which they live. On the contrary, they might receive a dose of ridicule and even intolerance. Actually, they're going to end up craving acceptance that's hard to come by; their bewildering appearance is not pleasant to look upon. They may seek to be viewed as normal; in fact, they are abnormal and that's the basic way the public is going to look upon them. All along in human history societies have looked with scorn upon men behaving as women and women behaving as men. The Old Testament forbade it.

Deuteronomy 22:5

The woman shall not wear that which pertains unto a man, neither shall a man put on a woman's garment: for all that do so are abomination unto the Lord your God.

Any clear-thinking person can easily recognize how out of place transgender practices are. A man may dress as a woman or a woman may dress like a man. They may seek to acquire the mannerisms of the opposite sex, but their behavior is just an affront, it's acting, it's a pretense. In the end, they will have failed in their effort to become the opposite sex and their attempts will have marred their bodies. They will have traveled a destructive road; they will have relinquished the possibility of regaining their God-given endowment. It is no wonder that suicide deaths rank high in the transgender community.

According to the Center for Disease Control, about 1 million people in the United States identify as transgenders; that's about 0.6% of the adult population. It is doubtful that their conclusion is reliable.[10]Nonetheless, the absurdity of this practice needs to be confronted from a clear-headed, honest, perspective.

Those individuals pursuing a sex change think they have the right to define their own identity. Just who granted them such an absurd right? Certainly not the God responsible for their given sex. In seeking to make such a change they discredit their God-given sex and lay a claim to what turns out to be an unrealistic, bogus, identity. Their freakish desires are against nature, against God, and against their physical bodies.

The loose cultural values of our American society have given plenty of space for weird behavior to emerge. The foundations of what is morally right and wrong are being trampled underfoot. Couples living together out of wedlock, homosexual marriage, and transgender operations are a few examples of standards that are far below par. Why would sound-thinking people ever make room for transgender practices to become a part of our culture? To do so will make ample room for satanic influence to thrive.

Some in the field of psychology have failed in their analysis of the transgender sex problem. They do so by giving legitimacy to the unwholesome, freakish, desires of individuals who are lusting for something they cannot have. When they do this they are facilitating the outlandish desires of their weak-minded patients. In the absence of spiritual savvy, a psychiatrist will fail to help their transgender patients. Transgenders may not get the help they seek from their counselors but they are sure to get a bill.

Parental failure to correct the freakish, unnatural, desires of their children is an indictment against their sanity and also their morality.[11] They have failed to help their offspring develop soundness in their thinking. They have allowed their children to skirt the sound judgment of reality. Those parents who have allowed this corrupted judgment to take root and grow in the minds of their boys and girls are behaving more like criminals than caring parents. They have abused their responsibility and also their parenthood. They are proving themselves to be spiritually corrupt. No morally minded parent would allow this weird, devilish, behavior to fester and grow in the minds and hearts of their sons and daughters.

Let us teach our children to be thankful for whom God has made them to be. Celebrate your daughter's femininity and your son's masculinity.

1 Answers in Genesis, Nov. 4, 2022, *When Trans People Regret Transitioning (Heartbreaking)* Youtube

2 Haeseker B., Nicolai JP, 01 Mar 2007, *The first gender changing operation from female to male in The Netherlands, 1959/'60*, Europe PMC

3 Gaffney, Theresa, Oct. 3, 2022, *History is Repeating Itself: The story of the nation's first clinic for gender-affirming surgery*, STAT News

4 The Oregonian, May 14, 2016, *Transgender health care horror stories*, YouTube

5 WBAL-TV 11 Baltimore, Sept. 9, 2015, *Gender reassignment surgery extremely complicated*, Youtube

6 Insider, July 10, 2019, *Transgender Americans Face Staggering Costs, Even With Health Insurance*, Youtube

7 Davis, Elliott, Jr., June 8, 2023, *States That Have Restricted Gender-Affirming Care for Trans Youth in 2023*, US News

8 Statista, June 6, 2023, *Suicide rate of transgender people in the United States in 2022,* by sex assigned at birth, Statista Research Dept.

9 DocuBay Documentaries, March 30, 2023, *Transgenders Regret 'Sex Change' Surgery, Watch Them Share Their Experience To Create Awareness,* Youtube

10 Division of HIV Prevention, National Center for HIV, Viral Hepatitis, STD, and TB Prevention, Centers for Disease Control and Prevention, March 23, 2023 *HIV and Transgender People, CDC*

11 The Daily Signal, June 13, 2023, *Grieving Mom on Radical Transgender Bill: "I don't want any parent to feel what I feel every day",* Youtube

CHAPTER 6

THE CLIMATE CHANGE HOAX

The lively debate around climate change continues to occupy center stage in our modern-day society. Climate change propaganda has developed a broad following. A large segment of our population has bought into the dubious concept that they think is real. Are the proponents of climate change right? If they're wrong, the sooner we can discover their error, the better. We need to look behind their doomsday message and discover the motives behind what they are proclaiming.

We have not yet mastered the universe, and the planets remain far beyond our capacity to search them out. We can barely comprehend the vast distance of our universe. Closer to home, here on Earth, we're still searching out the mysteries of creation. We have not mastered the seas, and we have not mastered the weather. It is sad to say, but the human species can barely govern themselves. Murder, theft, rape, millions in prison, and vicious deadly wars are a testament to that reality.

A good example of what is being said is our love affair with cars. We boast and glory in our automobiles. But take a good look at how they have caused so much injury and harm to human life. Cars do help us to get there faster; but, is getting there faster more important than the lives of the millions who've died in automobile crashes? To quote an old jingle, "We've come a long way baby but we still have a long way to go."

It could well be that a correct analysis of how Earth's atmosphere functions is beyond our capacity to completely understand it. God, who created the atmosphere, asks the following of Job knowing that Job could not respond positively.

Job 38:33

Know you the ordinances of heaven? Can you set the dominion thereof in the earth?

The depth of our understanding concerning the ordinances of the heavens remains incomplete. Generally speaking, the scientific method has been a useful and productive tool. The human species has benefited highly as a result of scientific discoveries. Our Heavenly Father has given the human species a great mental capacity for investigating and discovering. However, that cannot justify patting ourselves on the back. The scientific community also has a history of numerous big-time blunders. At one time scientists thought the Earth was the center of the universe. Our first president, George Washington, was bled to death by the scientific medical practices of his day. In our day, the scientists at Wuhan, China developed the deadly COVID virus that has killed millions around the world. Who is the scientist among us that can tell the number of stars in the heavens or the number of sand on the seashores? So, the trial and error method of science sometimes works well but sometimes its conclusions are harmful.

We have been schooled to "TRUST THE SCIENCE." Trusting the science is fine if it is kept to the things in which science is competent. When science is regarded as the only way to truth and other options are not counted to have validity then we are on very shaky ground. That science is the only way to truth is false. Science cannot investigate the Gospel of the Lord Jesus Christ to prove it true or false.

I Corinthians 2:14

But the natural man receives not the things of the Spirit of God: for they are foolishness unto him: neither can he know them, because they are spiritually discerned.

Science cannot answer the meaningful questions of a little child; Where did I come from? Where will I end up? What is the meaning of my life? Science just cannot answer the most important questions about life; it can't tell you what you "ought" to do. It is God's Word that teaches us what we ought to do. We need the Bible to answer the bigger questions about life.

FAR-OUT LIBERALS

Annually, a select group of individuals gathers in Davos, Switzerland to attend the World Economic Forum. Most of those in attendance could be classified as the "Liberal Elite" who are without scientific credentials. Some of them in attendance say that they are seeking to save planet Earth. Their speeches deliver doomsday prophecies of the Earth's future demise.

The devil can work its mischievous purposes through some of their bloated egos. Their arrogance has prompted them to imagine vain things, and they authoritatively spout their conclusions. They are truly staunch proponents of climate change theory. However, even the casual observer can see their hypocrisy. They continue to fly their private planes around the world. They continue to drive their carbon-emitting cars. They continue to heat their homes with fossil fuels. The contradiction between what they say and what they do is so obvious. Their motives are highly questionable. It's hard to believe what they are saying because we can see just what they are doing! And if their conclusions are wrong, their prophecies of Earth's doom have generated fear in the hearts of the simple and gullible. Who knows, maybe some of their ancestry dates back to "Chicken Little?"

OPPOSITION TO DOOMSDAY PROPHETS

The testimonies of an increasing number of renowned scientists, from around the World, are voicing their opposition to doomsday climate change projections. In the year 2015, Dr. Steven F Hayward, a professor at Berkley University, addressed a group gathered at Hillsdale College in Michigan. The title of his address was, "A Funny Thing Happened On The Way To Global Warming." Dr. Hayward brought to light some of the errors of scientific climate change computer models. His address pointed out some of the following: during the period between 1979 to 1998, the global average temperature rose 0.4 tenths of a degree Celsius. This fell in line with computer model predictions. After 1998, for the next twenty-plus years, the warming suddenly stopped. Consequently, all of the computer models were becoming falsified. 95% of model predictions proved to be wrong. If that trend were to continue (and it did) close to 100% of the models would be proven wrong.[1] Erroneous predictions have become an embarrassment to the scientist responsible for making them.

Additionally, Dr. Hayward reported that John Cook from Queensland, Australia, after having reviewed summaries of 11,000 scientific papers, reported that two-thirds of all the papers reported nothing about climate change being caused by human intervention. 97% of the remaining papers (that is only one-third) supported the position that humans were the cause of climate change warming. We need to be clear about this matter. The present-day information that 97% of all scientists believe that climate change is caused by human intervention is a falsehood. That falsehood began by misrepresenting John Cook's report. The truth is, 97% of scientists do not believe that climate change is caused by human intervention.

Dr.John Christy, an atmospheric professor at the University of Alabama, gave his testimony before a congressional climate change committee in 2015.

Dr. Christy's work includes the building of climate test models from scratch. He's highly qualified in this field of endeavor. His report emphasized that climate models are often less than reliable. He does not believe that we understand the Earth's climate well enough to predict the certainty of its behavior. He does not believe the climate is broken; or that there is a climate crisis.[2]

In a European Climate Declaration addressed to the United Nations, dated September 26, 2019, 500 scientists agreed that there is no climate emergency. The letter encouraged more moderation on both the parts of scientists and political leaders. The website, climatechangereconsiderewd.org, list the reports of the Nongovernmental International Panel On Climate Change (NIPCC). Their website list the works of a large number of climate scientists who refute the view of the diehard climate activists. Their research proves that the climate change doctrine is not "settled science."

Dr. Richard Lindzen started his climate research back in the1970's. During his work as an atmospheric physicist, he published well over 200 scientific papers and books. His outstanding research has led him to openly challenge climate change activists. He calls them climate change alarmists. He calls their outspoken assertions scientifically unrealistic. The scientific climate models, which they hold in such high esteem, he disputes. Dr. Lindzen believes the climate change alarmist have a hidden agenda; they have a quest for power. If they control the source of Earth's energy they can exercise control over the people of the world.[3] The process for that coming to pass is underway.

POLITICAL TREACHERIES

Many of today's politicians and lawmakers have embraced climate change theory. They are persuaded about its truth and they have become sold-out believers. However, the shaky foundation of climate change predictions, which our political leaders are relying upon, is absolutely a false premise. It is not only false, it is absurd! These same individuals have assumed an unquestionable, authoritarian, stance that will not be denied. Nonetheless, human activity is not the cause of climate change. God built climate change into the structure of how the Earth is to behave.

It is past time that we start thinking about the horrific damage climate change activist are heaping upon our lives. They are taking our citizenship freedoms and casting the crippling power of fear against us. The roughshod methods by which lawmakers are destroying the industries of their opponents (fossil fuel and coal and still others) certainly bring to bear legitimate questions. What are their motives and intentions? In the deep recesses of their hearts, what are they up to? What are they trying to achieve? Have they utilized the fears and dismays generated by false scientific conclusions to aid their financial endeavors? One might wonder how are they profiting personally from the laws and regulations they are enacting. Why is it they have little or no concern about the coal workers and fossil fuel personnel that they are damaging? How is it that some of their relatives, friends, and business acquaintances secure lucrative contracts to build the components of their "green agenda?" These and other questions still need honest forthright answers. To quote Honest Abe: "You can fool some of the people some of the time, and most of the people most of the time, but not all of the people all of the time." Are ardent climate change activists "righteous warriors" who will save the Earth, or are they self-seeking men and women feathering their pockets with ill-gotten gain? Maybe we would do well to take a close look and see if their pockets are sagging low while they are on the way to making their bank deposits.

WHAT THE MEDIA DUMPS

The national news media was never appointed to their lofty positions by legitimate institutions. If they were held responsible for what they report, things would go better for them and us also. For the most part, they are self-appointed individuals that claim they are serving the public's "right to know". However, their tainted climate change news leads the public astray. Instead of printing the truth about climate change they print and broadcast their liberal-minded beliefs about the subject. Just whom are they fooling? The national news media, both TV and newspapers, hunger for juicy information to foster the causes of outspoken liberals; of whom they largely are a part. Their news reporting supports climate change theory, hook-line-and-sinker! When have they ever been neutral-minded with their reporting? Not very often. So, don't shake hands with the enemy, thinking that they're trustworthy. It's so obvious, for the most part, our national media is the stretched-out arm of a highly liberal political party. What they report about climate change is highly biased. They are sold-out believers who have embraced the dark view of Earth's demise. Many of them are high-minded liberals who reject the truth and accuracy of the Word of God. Their contrary doomsday views are highly damaging to the public. They are not seekers of truth, but rather they seek to perpetuate falsehoods about the demise of planet Earth. Their hidden, impure, motives have become a stench in the nostrils of sound-thinking Americans.

SPIRITUAL INSIGHT AND ENLIGHTENMENT

We need to consider how our Heavenly Father fits into the subject of climate change. Our examination of this highly charged issue must be viewed from a spiritual perspective. Without the dimension of the spiritual view, seriously false conclusions will lead to disastrous consequences. The argument is not between climate change science being right or wrong. Rather, it is between what climate change scientists have concluded and what God has proclaimed in His Word.

The reality is that every good and perfect gift comes down to us by the grace, mercy, and goodness of our Creator.

James 1:16-18

Do not err, my beloved brethren. Every good gift and every perfect gift is from above, and cometh down from the Father of lights, with Whom is no variableness, neither shadow of turning. Of His own will begat He us with the word of truth, that we should be a kind of first fruits of His creatures.

What we need to recognize is that God has placed the rainbow in Earth's atmosphere for a purpose. The presence of the rainbow in the sky is a token of His promise concerning Earth, and its inhabitants. He has promised that the Earth will never again be destroyed by a flood; it will endure. After a rain, the bow becomes plainly evident before our eyes.

Genesis 9:16

And the bow shall be in the cloud; and I will look upon it, that I may remember the everlasting covenant between God and every living creature of all flesh that is upon the earth.

The everlasting covenant God has established with the Earth, and the people in it, is ongoing. It's still in affect; it will not cease. For our purposes, the part of this covenant that needs to be emphasized is the following promise God has made to Earth's people.

Genesis 8:22

While the earth remaineth, seedtime and harvest, and cold and heat, and summer and winter, and day and night shall not cease.

While the Earth remains, seedtime and harvest, and cold and heat, and summer and winter, and day and night shall not cease until when? Earth is going to endure until it is destroyed by fervent heat as described by the following Scripture:

II Peter 3:10

But the day of the Lord will come as a thief in the night; in the which the heavens shall pass away with a great noise, and the elements shall melt with fervent heat, the earth also and the works that are therein shall be burned up.

The day described in this verse will come at the end of the book of Revelation period, and the thousand-year millennial reign of Jesus Christ.[4] The destruction of the Earth will not come about by the hands of men's poor stewardship. This destruction will come about just as it is described and outlined by the most trustworthy book on planet Earth. The following Scripture references teach how God sustains night and day. They also teach that He sustains the ordinances of Heaven and Earth.

Jeremiah 33:20-21a

Thus saith the Lord; If you can break My covenant of the day, and My covenant of the night, and that there should not be day and night in their season; Then may also My covenant be broken with David, My servant.

Jeremiah 33:25-26a

Thus saith the Lord; If My covenant be not with day and night, and if I have not appointed the ordinances of heaven and earth; Then will I cast away the seed of Jacob, and David My servant.

God could break the covenants He's made with men and women, but He never will; because they are steadfast and enduring. Men and women have broken their covenant standing with God, but God always upholds the covenant promises He has made with His people. God is not a man that He should lie. God's covenant concerning day and night is that they will endure. By this time it should be clear that the time frame for the end of the Earth rests with God Almighty.

He alone appointed the ordinances of Heaven and Earth and the time frame for their endurance.

I Samuel 2:8b

For the pillars of the earth are the Lord's, and He has set the world upon them.

II Peter 3:6-7

Whereby the world that then was, being overflowed with water, perished: but the heavens and the Earth, which are now, by the same word are kept in store, reserved unto fire against the day of judgment and perdition of ungodly men.

It is true that men and women are wasteful and sometimes inconsiderate of the outstanding provisions God has placed in their care. However, their lack of stewardship, though harmful, will not bring about Earth's demise. Yes, God wants us to be good stewards of what He has created. Stewardship is taking care of the resources and assets our Creator has placed in our hands. The beauty and utility of Earth's resources do belong to us. Their care and keeping are our responsibility; so we must guard against their abuse. However, man's behavior does not trump God's promises.

TWO OPINIONS

So, now the question has become whose word are we going to believe? Will we believe the trustworthy word of our loving Heavenly

Father, the Creator of Heaven and Earth; or will we believe the words of men who have imagined vain things? Scientific theories and findings cannot negate the order and standing of God Almighty. We know what God has promised He will do.

Human extinction is not within the care and keeping of Earth's people. God is in control of Earth's keeping. The end time of the Earth, as we know it, is clearly defined in the Scriptures. Nowhere does Scripture teach that human existence will be smothered out by a lack of oxygen or too much carbon dioxide. Again, the fervent heat destruction of the earth, referred to biblically, comes after the millennial (1,000-year) reign of the Lord Jesus Christ and not before. This great reality is proof positive that climate change is a hoax. It is a false, devilish, doctrine that contradicts the living Word of God. Jesus Christ referred to the Earth's passing away:

> **Matthew 24:35-36**
>
> **Heaven and earth shall pass away, but my words shall not pass away. But of that day and hour knows no man, no, not the angels of Heaven, but My Father, only.**

THE DEVIL'S WORK

Climate change is much more than a man-made scientific theory. Sadly, today it is accepted as truth when it is in fact a deceptive lie. This acceptance has made adequate room for the devil to work its scheming devices. The devilish harm that it is working upon our nation is truly deplorable. Entire industries are being destroyed. Their employees are suffering crippling financial loss. Our school children are intimidated by doomsday fears. Words of truth concerning Earth's existence are being belittled and ignored.

Vast amounts of revenue are being ripped from the pockets of the American public. Their money is financing a bogus climate change agenda. This absurd agenda is presently being cast upon our citizenry by a dictatorial government. Their strong-handed influence is working hardship upon our people. What they are dishing out is undermining the freedom values we are expecting them to protect. Sadly, our governmental leadership will not allow any debate to take place. They deny the legitimacy of any opponent. They are simply ignoring their critics. They are hell-bent on trying to shove their green agenda purposes down the throats of our people. Do they know what is better for us than we do? They mistakenly think so. They claim to be "Angels of Light" but their works are casting darkness and despair upon our nation. Even the devil seeks to appear as an Angel of Light.

The Bible's standard for good judgment was told by Jesus Christ, "You shall know them by their fruits." Can you see how this climate change mania is a devilish influence upon the minds and hearts of our society? It's working the plan and purposes of our adversary, the devil; its work is to steal, kill, and destroy. This unwholesome, devilish, climate change doctrine seeks to destroy the promises of a loving God. But we are wise to the devil's devices. God's promises include wondrous care and protection for His people. He watches over us day-by-day. His eternal purposes will come to pass despite our adversary's efforts to the contrary.

The Earth will end when God says it will end. That decision is in His care and keeping. His time frame is spelled out in His Matchless Word. If the human species were capable of destroying the planet maybe they would have done so before this time. God created the atmosphere even before He created man. He established the systems that have sustained it. He has given the people of the Earth a wholesome environment that has lasted century after century. That's not going to change until His eternal purposes are fulfilled. The climate change hoax must be recognized for what it truly is. It's diametrically opposed to the promises of God's unchangeable Word. It's a doctrine of devils, which undermines our economy and our hopes for a brighter life here in The United States. God is always good. He placed the oil fields under Earth's surface for a purpose. That purpose includes the betterment of Earth's people.

As long as the upright people of this land stand by in silence nothing will change. The promoters of the climate change hoax will have their way. God's people need to get better informed about this issue. Then, they can begin to shout the truth into the public arena. They can commence to confront those who have bought into the climate change hoax. Before the shackles of this climate change doctrine can be fully removed, the citizenry of our nation must look to God for His help; He can bring marvelous things to pass.

Again, the underlying issues about climate change must be viewed from a spiritual perspective. It is when the spiritual aspect surrounding the climate change doctrine is brought to the forefront that its evil intent becomes fully evident.

1 Hayward, Steven F. Pepperdine University, Nov. 11, 2014, *A Funny Thing Happened on the Way to Global Warming*, Youtube

2 BizNewsTv, Dec. 12, 2022, *Data shows there's no climate catastrophe looming - climatologist Dr. J. Christy debunks the narrative*, Youtube

3 BizNewsTv, April 20, 2023, *Dr. Richard Lindzen exposes climate change as a politicized power play motivated by malice and profit*, Youtube

4 Matthew 24:29-31

CHAPTER 7

ARE THE DEAD ALIVE AND IN HEAVEN?

It's true, millions of Christian believers still believe the dead are alive and living in heaven. Some of them have come to this misunderstanding by relying upon their earthbound knowledge. They have heard others all through the years teach this mistaken conclusion. Why do they accept such a misguided conclusion? Is it that they just can't accept the idea of a loved one lying in a dark enclosed casket, six feet under the earth? Maybe they mistakenly think their departed loved one retains some form of consciousness; that their spirit remains alive and trapped under the earth. Their real problem is that they are not giving due consideration to what the Scriptures actually teach. So, this false teaching has become easier for them to accept. It has become a weak crutch for them to lean upon. The deception they have adopted has led them into serious error.

It is a lying, devilish, doctrine that the dead are alive and living in heaven. That the dead are alive now and living in heaven is more than a mistaken assumption; it is a denial of what our Bible teaches about this subject. The wonderful Christian believers who have been misled by this false idea can find real solace by carefully considering what the Bible actually teaches. The purpose of this chapter is not to condemn those who believe the dead are alive. It is rather to help them see the clarity of Scriptures they may have not understood. When Scriptures dealing with the truth of this subject are brought to light, new vistas of understanding are easy to grasp. John 8:32 states, " And you shall know the truth and the truth shall make you free."

There is a problem here that needs to be resolved. When Christian believers say that their departed loved one is alive and in heaven they are contradicting the plain, obvious, and accurate teaching listed below:

1 Thessalonians 4:13-17

But I would not have you to be ignorant, brethren, concerning them which are asleep, that you sorrow not, even as others which have no hope. For if we believe that Jesus died and rose again, even so, them also which sleep in Jesus will God bring with him. For this we say unto you by the word of the Lord, that we which are alive and remain unto the coming of the Lord, shall not prevent (that is precede) them which are asleep. For the Lord himself shall descend from heaven with a shout, with a voice of the archangel, and with the trump of God: and the dead in Christ shall rise first:

Then we which are alive and remain, shall be caught up together with them in the clouds, to meet the Lord in the air: and so shall we ever be with the Lord.

The word "asleep" in the above verses is used as a synonym for the word "dead." The word sleep is meant to be a more comforting word. In sleep, there is no consciousness. The same is true concerning the dead. The dead are without memory and therefore without consciousness. They will remain in that state of unconsciousness until they are resurrected by the command of the Lord Jesus Christ. Then (and not until then) Christian believers will be raised with incorruptible new bodies and will at that time regain consciousness.

The clear words of the above Scripture are "the Lord himself shall descend from heaven and the dead in Christ shall rise first" and those still alive on Earth "shall be caught up together with them (with the dead) in the clouds to meet the Lord in the air." The emphatic truth of these verses is stated so plainly that no one needs to miss it. The dead will get to Heaven when Jesus Christ calls them to everlasting life.

I Corinthians 15:42-44

So also, is the resurrection of the dead. It is sown in corruption; it is raised in incorruption: It is sown in dishonor; it is raised in glory: It is sown in weakness; it is raised in power: It is sown a natural body; it is raised a spiritual body. There is a natural body, and there is a spiritual body.

The departed dead will remain in the state of death until they are resurrected. Obviously, the dead can't be alive in heaven and in the grave at the same time. The trustworthy Scriptures above tell the story. The dead remain in the unconscious state of death until the glorious voice of Jesus Christ raises them and they receive their new incorruptible bodies. Again, then (and not until then) they will be with the Lord Jesus Christ and spend everlasting life with him.

The above passages of Scripture are not isolated testimonies of where the dead now reside. Many other related Scriptures testify to the truth we are examining here. Below is an even fuller account!

I Corinthians 15:51-54

Behold, I show you a mystery; we shall not all sleep, but we shall all be changed, in a moment, in the twinkling of an eye, at the last trump: for the trumpet shall sound, and the dead shall be raised incorruptible, and we shall be changed. For this corruptible must put on incorruption, and this mortal must put on immortality. So when this corruptible shall have put on incorruption, and this mortal shall have put on immortality, then shall be brought to pass the saying that is written, "Death is swallowed up in victory."

The only true source of information concerning the actual state of the dead is the message of the Christian Bible. All other sources are from earthbound knowledge and are without spiritual savvy. So, whom will you believe - the earthbound knowledge of corruptible men, or the truthfully accurate word of our Heavenly Father?

If one believes other sections of Scripture about this subject are true, then one can't throw the ones presented above to one side in unbelief. If it is true that all other Scriptures are true then the ones above are also true! No one should pick and choose which part of the Word of

God they will believe; it's "either or". Either you accept all the Word of God to be true, or you fail to believe some other parts are true. The integrity of God's Word is absolute; it's not hit-and-miss. What God says in His Word is exactly what God intended to say. Our job is to work through passages that seem to be contradictory and find the accuracy of the original word spoken and written by holy men of God.

The scope of this book cannot treat all the controversial Scriptures that seemingly teach that the dead are alive now. Dr. Victor Paul Wierwille in his little book, *Are The Dead Alive Now,* presents his marvelous research on seemingly contradictory Scriptures. On the surface, these Scriptures may seem to teach that the dead are alive now and living in Heaven. His research unravels the misunderstanding surrounding these Scriptures. Some of the misunderstood passages of Scripture he addresses are as follows:

Philippians I:12-27, II Corinthians 5:8-9, Matthew 17:1-9, Hebrews 11:5, Luke 16:19-31, Luke 23:42-43, Matthew 22:23-32 and I Samuel 28:7-25

There is a common mistaken belief that science can fathom life in the spiritual realm. However, science is actually limited to information that can be ascertained by the five senses. Five senses perception cannot bridge the fixed gap between the physical and the spiritual. Scientific endeavors in this field are a waste of time. The findings they seek to prove remain questionable. Please don't expect that their efforts in the spiritual category will be a fruitful undertaking.

In this category, fake science has opened up the demented activity of spiritualism. The devilish doctrine that "the dead are alive now" is straight from Satan's tool chest. Satan can and does counterfeit phenomenon that appears to be genuine. In seances and other "hookie-pook" activities like extrasensory perception activity, devilish powers counterfeit the dead and can make them appear to be alive. The unsuspecting and gullible grab on to these delusions and believe them to be true. The reality is, this kind of activity adds up to the devil's false proof "that the dead are alive." Christian believers need to rise up and steer clear of this entrapment. The devil's tricky devices will become obvious when God's people turn on their spiritual perception and awareness. (James 4:7) "Submit yourselves therefore to God. Resist the devil, and he (it) will flee from you".

The important thing for us to understand is that we can count on the complete accuracy of what the Bible teaches concerning life after death. Our Heavenly Father will not leave us in the grave. God has prepared us with the truthful information we need concerning death. There is no need to remain doubtful about it. Death is an enemy, but we have the promise of the Lord Jesus Christ that he will resurrect us to live again with him. Yes, we are going to live again with all the wonderful believers who are born of God's spirit. There is no need for us to fear death. We are absolutely comforted by what God has taught. Our eyes have been enlightened. We are not without hope, as others who have no hope. Praise God! One day, the Lord Jesus Christ will appear in the clouds to call us to our new Heavenly Home. He will gather us together to be with him, and so "we shall ever be with the Lord". Until that day comes we can joy and rejoice; we are Heaven bound.

CHAPTER 8

THE DOCTRINE OF THE TRINITY

During the years I spent in theology school questions about the Trinity were often discussed with fellow students. Everybody seemed to have their own opinion; some believed one thing, and others believed something different. I could not figure it out. To me, "God the Son" thinking undermined and belittled the wondrous accomplishments of the man Jesus Christ. It was his manhood and strength of character that made him shine like a light. He walked and talked with his Heavenly Father for guidance and strength. He said of himself, "I can't do anything of myself." He totally trusted in God his Father. For those of us who could not figure it out we were encouraged to take it by faith. I decided to place the teaching of the Trinity to one side. My view was that, if I could remain patient over this issue, eventually, I could gain a clear understanding about the accuracy or falsehood of this Trinitarian doctrine.

I doubt that anyone would call me an outstanding biblical scholar; neither am I a novice. I started training for the Christian Ministry at the age of twenty. I graduated from three institutions of higher learning. Most of the classes I attended were subjects dealing with theology and pastoral training. Over the years of my life, I served as a pastor to several church congregations. I learned early on that the integrity of God's Word is absolute. I trust the Scriptures to say what they mean and to mean what they teach.

I am also aware that there are Scripture passages that appear to be contradictory to one another. Many of these passages are the results of bogus translations. Some of them have been complicated by the inserted opinions of scribes and monks. Without a doubt, it does take diligent study and meekness of heart, to clear up controversial Scriptures. The original "God-breathed Word" given to holy men of God was perfectly pinned. Now the work of Christian believers must be to search out the meaning of the Scriptures originally given by the inspiration of God.

Eventually, in my last year of theology school, I was introduced to a book written by Dr. Victor Paul Wierwille.[1] The title of his book is *Jesus Christ Is Not God*. At first, I thought Dr. Wierwille was trying to pick a fight with the popular view of the Trinity. However, after having met him, and looking carefully at his research and teachings I became convinced that this godly man was not a crackpot seeking to pick a fight against traditional views. The more I studied his research the more I became convinced that he had brought to light the information I had sought for years. The clarity of how he treated controversial Scriptures surrounding the doctrine of the Trinity was outstanding. He has been able to unravel the twisted, controversial, Scriptures that, on the surface, seemed to justify teachings about the Trinity. For those who are not fully persuaded about the truthfulness of the Trinity, I highly recommend Dr. Wierwille's research. I have benefited highly by having known him and having studied his tremendous research. No longer am I confused about this important subject; praise God! The clarity I sought for so many years has given me the straightforward information to come to the best conclusion.

Questions surrounding the validity of the Trinity doctrine have been voiced since the third century AD. Christian believers have remained divided by this doctrine up to the present. It is with a true sense of humility that I approach the treatment of this chapter. I recognize what a touchy, sensitive, subject this is among the various groups and denominations that make up the Christian Community. This author's job is not to take a militant stance against the doctrine of the Trinity. It is rather from a spirit of humility to share the views that I have accumulated during the last five decades of my life. We are taught by the Word of God to be especially kind to the household of faith. We who are born-again of God's spirit make up the wonderful Body of Christ. Together we are God's people and we all belong to the Family of God. So, let's put away our squabbling and condemnation of each other.

Romans 12: 9-10

Let love be without dissemination. Abhor that which is evil; cleave to that which is good. Be kindly affectioned one to another with brotherly love; in honor preferring one another.

CHRISTIAN DIVISION

There are a few isolated Scriptures that, on the surface, seem to teach that Jesus Christ may be God. However, the vast majority of the New Testament record says nothing about Jesus Christ being God. When we look at the first-hand witnesses of the life of Jesus Christ he's referred to in many ways, but never do these witnesses say he's God. Mary, the mother of Jesus, never referred to her son as God. Surely, she knew the essence of the child to whom she had given birth. God's personal message to Mary, delivered by the angle Gabriel, informed this wonderful woman that her son "shall be called, The Son of God" (Luke 1:26-35). The following individuals knew him personally. The brothers and sisters of Jesus never called him God. They on one occasion even contradicted his spirituality. His family traveled to Capernaum to take him home (Matthew12:46). They thought him to be "beside himself" i.e., out of touch with reality.

The apostles never called Jesus, God. It's true that Thomas, seeing the resurrected body of Jesus Christ, referred to him as "my godly Lord", (John 20:28) but that is different than addressing him as God.

Matthew 16:13-15

When Jesus came into the coasts of Caesarea Philippi, he asked his disciples saying, "Whom do men say that I, the son of man am? And they said, "Some say that you are John the Baptist: some Elias; and others, Jeremiah or one of the prophets." He said unto them, "But whom say you that I am?" And Simon Peter answered and said, "You are the Christ, the son of the living God."

THE DOCTRINE OF THE TRINITY

The Apostle Nathanael referred to Jesus as, "the Son of God."[2] However, not one single disciple of Jesus Christ ever referred to him as a deity. John the Baptist's testimony of Jesus Christ is perfectly clear:

> **John 1:32-34**
>
> **And John bare record, saying, "I saw the Spirit descending from heaven like a dove, and it abode upon him. And I knew him not: but He that sent me to baptize with water, the same said unto me, 'Upon whom you shall see the Spirit descending, and remaining on him, the same is he which baptizes with the holy ghost.' And I saw, and bare record that this is the son of God."**

The Pharisees were very upset with Jesus when he referred to himself as the son of God. Even devil spirits called Jesus, "the son of God."

These were the individuals who knew Jesus best; they were first-hand eyewitnesses; they knew him personally. What they reported of him is the most authentic information available. The first references describing Jesus as God came much later than the First Century AD.

The idea of Jesus Christ being co-equal with God gained support early in the 4th century. Bishop Alexander, of Alexandria Egypt, along with other bishops, supported the following belief. They claimed that God can do anything He chooses, so God incarnated Himself – He became human; He chose to become Jesus. Only if Jesus was fully human could he atone for human sin and only if he was fully divine could he have the power to save us.

Arius, a priest, also from Alexandria Egypt, believed that God adopted Jesus as His son, but that did not mean they were equal. He believed that Jesus of Nazareth was a real man, not some divine aberration of God, or God for that matter.[3] Years later, the church council at Constantinople in the year 381 AD reaffirmed the Nician Council of 325 AD. The Trinitarian doctrine established then is embraced today by a large segment of the Christian Community. Most of the doctrine is stated below:

> We believe in one God, the Father Almighty, Maker of all things visible and invisible and in one Lord Jesus Christ, the Son of God, the only - begotten of the Father, of the substance (homoousios) of the Father; God of God and Light of Light; true God of true God; begotten, not made, of the same substance as the Father, by whom all things were made, in heaven and on earth: who for the sake of us men and our salvation, descended, became incarnate, and was made man, suffered, arose again on the third day, and ascended into the heavens, from where he will come again to judge the living and the dead; and in the Holy Spirit.

SEPARATING BRETHREN

It is not within the framework of this book to give a detailed historical accounting of how the doctrine of the Trinity came to us today. Several authors have already presented this information. For example, Richard E. Rubenstein, a professor at George Mason University, does a good job of this in his book, *When Jesus Became God.*[4] The emphasis I hope to highlight centers more around how our adversary, the devil, utilizes the doctrine of the Trinity as a wedge to separate brethren.

One piece of history we do need to look at more closely centers around what developed in and around the church council which met at Nicaea in 325 AD. The Roman emperor, Constantine, convened the council with the expectation of developing unity among the hundreds of independent bishops ruling the Christian Community at that time. At the emperor's behest, the council pinned the doctrine Constantine wanted. However, their doctrine of the Trinity failed to produce unity. What it did foster was divisions, hatred, and even savage murders. The emperor having intervened in a religious debate made it possible for the Trinitarian bishops to levy political power.

It is not that those militant bishops were more qualified to define the identity of Christ. There is no record of any of these bishops having met with Jesus first hand. However, with the power of the emperor at their disposal, they could force their views upon dissenters. They set out to thwart any opposition to their dogmatic stance. The council's conclusion stated that "Jesus Christ was very God of very God." Now having the power of the emperor backing them up, militant bishops began to war against the opposing bishops who would not comply with the council's conclusion. Maybe they did not understand that pleasing the emperor and pleasing God were two different things. Their constant use of non-biblical terms like "substance", "equal ", and "essence" in defining Jesus raised the eyebrows of those who did not believe the Trinitarian doctrine to be true.

It wasn't that the dissenters against the council's conclusion were pagan God-rejecters. They were, in fact, brethren with a different belief about the person of Christ. Nor were they militants, wheeling their swords of righteousness and thrusting them into the bodies of their opponents. This is a closer description of those who supported the council's decision. The vehement attitudes they displayed against their brethren are clearly an indication that they were not, in fact, qualified to decide the true nature of Christ's identity.

Theophilus, the fire-breathing bishop of Alexandria, incited local vigilantes to destroy the Temple of Serapis, one of the largest and most beautiful buildings in the ancient world, with a library donated by Cleopatra. Alexandrian Christians whipped up by Bishop Cyril rioted against the Jews in 415, and then murdered Hypatia, a wise and beloved Platonic philosopher.[5]

The above description, of this horrific violence, is indicative of what occurred after the Council of Nicene ended. The go-signal had been given to the "Jesus Is God followers." They openly branded anyone differing from their, supposed, validated views. Little by little, their opponents were excommunicated, banished, assaulted, and demeaned. Violent eruptions against dissenters continued to flare up decades, and even centuries, after the politically influenced decision at Nicene.

It is not surprising that the triumph of Nicene Christianity was followed by a violent campaign to impose the new order on outsiders. Other revolutionary movements once consolidated internally, have turned aggressively against unbelievers still "outside the walls."(i.e. outside of their doctrinal belief)[6]

One historian wrote that: "bishop was contending against bishop, and the people were contending against one another, like swarms of gnats fighting in the air." Church Council meeting after Council meeting attests to the reality that nothing was settled concerning the three-in-one doctrine. It was not settled in the fourth-century councils; nor has it ever been truly settled.

Here we are in the 21st century and this devilish controversy persists. Christian brethren remain separated over the proper identity of Christ Jesus who surely loves them all. Those who are proponents of the Trinity will not allow questions from their opponents; rather they brand them to be radical members of a cult. Distrust, fear, thinking evil, and ridicule are attitudes displayed towards fellow brethren. Even family members are shunned by one another. Opponents are generally excluded from fellowship. So the doctrine of the Trinity has now become a test of faith; you are either "in" or you're "out". "Out" in the sense of banishment, or withdrawal of fellowship.

Those who are today so staunch to confess the doctrine of the Trinity might be repulsed by the almighty bishops who worked their murderous wills upon hundreds of those they defined to be their opponents. We may not be completely able to understand all the motives of those bishops governing the churches in the third and fourth centuries AD. but, we can understand their actions. The despicable treatment they levied against fellow believers is completely out of harmony with even the rudimentary practices of New Testament Christianity. Those militant bishops' aggressive behavior did not exemplify the teachings of Jesus Christ. Their actions truly cast a doubt on their ability to properly define the nature and person of our Lord Jesus Christ. The cruelty they cast upon their opposition did not mirror the actions of the loving Savior's "person" they sought to define.

Jesus defined the actions of Satan as a thief: "Satan comes to steal, kill, and destroy" (John 10:10). The militant behavior dozens of those Nicene bishops displayed matches up to the same description Jesus gave of Satan's behavior. The fruits of their behavior can be observed. They struck out viciously against those who opposed them. The crimes they committed against their brethren would today be punishable by death. Their wickedness is evident, and history has recorded it.

UNITARIAN BELIEFS

Those who deny that Jesus Christ is God have their own set of doctrinal beliefs. They are sometimes referred to as Biblical Unitarians. First and foremost, they believe God is one God and is not divided into three distinct Gods. They believe God created a seed in the womb of Mary. That's when the promised Messiah developed to become the only begotten Son of God. (No pre-existence other than in God's foreknowledge.) They believe Jesus was a true man born with perfect blood. He was never contaminated by sin. He walked perfectly before his Heavenly Father. The spirit of God was given to him in full measure. Through obedience, Jesus became the perfect sacrifice to pay for the sins of the world. In obedience to his Heavenly Father, he suffered death on a Roman cross. God raised him from the dead after three days and three nights. Today, he is in Heaven and is seated at God's right hand. Biblical Unitarians, just like Trinitarians, are staunch in their beliefs.

The mind-set of Biblical Unitarians is that when people look upon Jesus Christ and believe that he is God, they belittle his accomplishment. God would have no problem being perfect. Also, if he was God then he could do whatever he chose to do. With this understanding, they may conclude; I'm not God; I can't do the mighty works that Jesus Christ did. However, if people believe Jesus was truly a man who trusted his Heavenly Father for power and guidance, then they too can follow his wonderful example and look to their Heavenly Father for power and guidance. Biblical Unitarians believes that "God the Son" thinking belittles the wondrous accomplishments of Jesus Christ. They believe it was his manhood, and strength of character, that made him shine like a light. He walked and talked with his Heavenly Father for guidance, strength, and know-how. He said of himself, "I can do nothing by myself." Truly he was a meek, faithful, loving, giving, selfless, man who trusted God with all his heart and soul. This is precisely what God asks of us.

Those who deny the Trinity's validity are often times seen looking down their noses at the mistaken ignorance of their Trinitarian brothers. They may be incensed at having been ostracized from Trinitarian fellowships. They think their differing opinion should be aired in the ears of those "died-in-the-wool" orthodox Trinitarians. Non-Trinitarians generally believe their counterparts are practicing idolatry by praying and worshipping Jesus who is the "Son of God" and not "God the Son."

Psalm 133

Behold, how good and how pleasant it is for brethren to dwell together in unity! It is like the precious ointment upon the head, that ran down upon the beard, even Aaron's beard: that went down to the skirts of his garments; as the dew of Hermon, and as the dew that descended upon the mountains of Zion: for there the Lord commanded the blessings, even life for evermore.

If the Corinthian Church could receive again a repentant man who had sexual intercourse with his father's wife surely each of us can tolerate different viewpoints about the identity of our Loving Savior. Once again, his love reaches all of us and he excludes none of us.

EXERCISING SPIRITUAL JUDGMENT

The fruits of a Trinitarian doctrine are not at all becoming. Brutal enforcement of the doctrine continued through the Protestant Reformation. The destruction it brought upon the community of Christian believers is appalling. Hundreds and hundreds of Christian men and women lost their lives at the hands of those leaders who ruled with devastating harshness. Fellow believers were tortured, banished, and cast into prison. It is obvious that satanic powers thrived amid ecclesiastic power gone astray.

Even from its inception the sour fruit of this ecclesiastical doctrine has pitted Church brother against Church brother. A wide divide among God's people continues over this issue. One could easily conclude, the doctrine of the Trinity has worked far more harm than good. The Orthodox Church leadership of our day allows little or no discussion of the Trinitarian belief. The doctrine of the Trinity cast upon believers long ago remains a devilish cancer that needs to be removed. Now is the right time to get rid of the harsh bitterness that hinders our Christian testimony.

Hindsight can be so revealing. Looking back, with the eyes of spiritual discernment, what occurred with the Nicene Council became the "devil's playground." The devil was able to work its purposes through the hard-hearted bishops that dominated the proceedings of the council. Actually, the mixture of politics and religion at the Nicene Council settled nothing; it complicated the atmosphere surrounding the true identity of Jesus Christ. The proceedings of the council set the stage for Satan to manipulate the heart-breaking separation of Christian Brethren. The devil's success in establishing a massive conflict concerning the true identity of Jesus has not ceased; it has lingered on. Biblical Unitarians cringe when they hear talk of a three-in-one God. They think the three-in-one doctrine focuses on a hypothetical idea that can't seriously be understood; it is not sensible. They can not take it by faith. Trinitarians condemn Unitarians as radical and call them a cult.

Let it be said, the devilish controversy over the identity of Jesus is a crippling testimony still churning and stirring within the Christian Community. It has separated the Body of Christ into hard-hearted divisions. It has robbed the Church of its unity and its strength. Arguments among brethren over the meaning of certain Scriptures seem to go on and on. Diverse interpretations continue to stoke the fires of division. To resolve the critical issues between them both sides need to measure up to what the Word of God teaches about the relationship between Christian brethren. Division, suspicions, condemnation, the withdrawal of fellowship, and thinking evil among Christians, needs to cease. This behavior is contrary to a Christian's character and standing. Please, replace those negative attitudes with compassion, open arms of forgiveness, preferring others before oneself, being tenderhearted, and loving each other with the love of God. It is the absence of all these uplifting qualities that invite Satan's intervention into the ongoing Trinitarian controversy. Creating discord among Christian brethren is a common tool utilized by satanic powers.

It is because individuals have elevated the doctrine of the Trinity above the importance of loving one another, that our defenses have failed against the works of Satan. We have failed to put on the protective armor God has provided.

Ephesians 6:10-13

Finally, my brethren, be strong in the Lord, and in the power of His might. Put on the whole armour of God, that you may be able to stand against the wiles of the devil. For we wrestle not against flesh and blood, but agains principalities, against powers, against the rulers of the darkness of this world, against spiritual wickedness in high places. Wherefore take unto you the whole armour of God, that you may be able to withstand in the evil day, and having done all, to stand.

A BETTER APPROACH

We truly need to remember who our real enemy is. Our enemy is not in the arena of the flesh and blood category. It is altogether in the spiritual realm. We are never to war against our brothers and sisters in the Lord. Our work is to bring deliverance and comfort to aid them in times of trouble. Since 17 centuries of debate have never settled the controversy; surely it's time for something better. It is time that Christian brethren take an altogether different approach to questions surrounding some of their church doctrines. Their attitudes and behavior need to reflect tolerance, friendship, understanding, patience, benevolence, and brotherly love, towards each other. Please, please, exhibit these! God is not, and will never be, pleased with a division among Christian believers. Unity and sanctification please Him.

Matthew 5:23-24

Therefore if you bring your gift to the altar, and there remember that your brother has something against you; leave there your gift before the altar, and go your way; first be reconciled to your brother, and then come and offer your gift.

Prayer for your Trinitarian brethren by Unitarians and prayer for your Unitarian brethren by Trinitarians will bring about wonderful change. The unity of heart-felt prayers will open doors of opportunity to minister to those with meekness to receive. God's guidance will give just the right answers for healing and deliverance to take place. God will reward our efforts with victory after victory. He will unlock doors that have been shut for too long. The hangover of a dark controversy between Christian brothers must be replaced with graceful reconciliation; this is an obtainable goal. Nothing short of loving grace and unity of heart can please our Heavenly Father. Merciful, peaceful, loving, words between us can get the job done. There is no need for delay. We can place our arguments to one side and sow a new crop of seed; one that will bring about the healing that is needed. Revival in our attitudes about each other will carry us to a peaceful place of unity.

1 Wierwille, Victor Paul, *Jesus Christ is Not God*, The American Christian Press, New Knoxville, Ohio, 1975

2 See John 1:49

3 *The Encyclopedia Britannica* 1968, s.v."Council of Nicaea"

4 Rubenstein, Richard E., *When Jesus Christ Became God*, Pub. Harcourt, Inc. N.Y., 1999

5 Ibid s.v. p.226

6 Ibid s.v. p226

CHAPTER 9

SUMMARY

This extended summary seeks to reinforce many of the prominent aspects covered in this book. Each topic discussed will appear above the subject.

SPIRIT LIFE

Even though Adam and Eve lost their spiritual nature, God prepared the way for us to receive the renewal of spirit life by Jesus Christ. The marvelous gift of spiritual life has made us into new creatures. We're no longer limited by earth-bound understanding. No longer do we walk in darkness, seeking the meaning of life. Now we understand who we are. We've gone far beyond our former natural-man existence. Now we walk with spiritual power and enlightenment. God's presence teaches and guides us into victorious living. Our spiritual awareness has opened up new dimensions of life. Daily we learn about the magnificence of our Heavenly Father. He has given us of His spirit. The purpose for our life is fully evident; we belong to God and our joy and purpose is to serve Him with all our heart.

We understand that God has empowered us with so much more than we had in the past. Word of knowledge, word of wisdom, discerning of spirits, and speaking in tongues, along with our other spiritual abilities, have given us the capacity to live victoriously. By our operation of these spiritual abilities we can minister to the needs of God's people. What a glory it is to walk in life with the power of God directing us.

It is the biblical view of life that has taught us who we truly are. It has taught us how the Words of God created the world; that He alone spoke the world and life into being. The Bible has also taught us how Adam and Eve were created with body, soul, and spirit. It has taught us how they lost their spiritual connection with God. Their rebellion against God brought the loss of their spirit life. They became limited to a body and soul existence.

LIFE WITHOUT HOLY SPIRIT

The Bible calls individuals who are without holy spirit "natural man". The natural-man of only body and soul is severely limited. They remain oblivious to spiritual realities. The "heavenly view" of life is beyond their comprehension. Their understanding is based only on experience and intelligence. Their biggest dilemma is their utter failure to recognize the purpose of their existence. Questions of how they got here and where they are going to end up are to them like peering through a dense fog. Natural-man's energies are primarily geared towards self-preservation. The way they treat others is defined mostly by their homespun philosophies. Their failure to get along with other people has led them into countless wars and rumors of wars. Their weird conclusions about the meaning of life, and the way they should conduct themselves, are found less speculations. They remain without hope because they have excluded the reality of a loving God.

To receive spirit life, the natural-minded can choose to love God. They can open up their minds to the excellency of God's presence, and choose to honor and obey Him. They can choose to accept God's calling so that they become born-again of His spirit. All of this is the process by which salvation and wholeness will come to their lives. In the next topic we are going to describe the biblical names of the evil spirit called the devil.

EVIL SPIRIT LIFE

The Bible fully describes an evil spiritual entity, one that's hostile to God. As we have seen this evil spiritual entity has been given several different names. The first one we discussed was Lucifer. Lucifer is described as being second only to God who created it. However, Lucifer's egocentric ambition caused its downfall. Now it seeks to reveal itself as an "Angel of Light." In other words, it's a "wolf in sheep's clothing." The wise-in-heart can recognize its ploys. Its rebellion against its Creator led directly to its being cast down to earth, and completely out of the heavenly realm. When this spirit was cast out of heaven it brought one-third of the angles with it. Even though Lucifer is called a serpent in Genesis chapter 3 that does not negate it also being an enticing, beautiful, bright, shining,

119

cherub. It did successfully entice Eve into rebellion against the promises of her Creator. That this frontal attack upon Eve was conducted by Satan is confirmed in the book of Revelation (chapter 12:9). There it is stated plainly that the old serpent is called the devil and Satan.

We do not need to remain ignorant of Satan's devices. The Bible record details the information we need to know about this evil spirit entity. Satan is also called an adversary; that is, an opposing spirit. The meaning of adversary has many different senses throughout Scripture. Some of these senses include; an enemy, to distress, to straighten, to bind, an accuser, an opponent, and to be in opposition. This adversarial spirit to God is therefore an adversarial spirit to God's people. As their accuser, this spirit seeks to keep God's people conscious of their sins and shortcomings. By hindering God's people, it hinders the plan of redemption initiated by our Creator.

Another name for this spirit is the devil. This spirit has set about to destroy the true God and Father of our Lord Jesus Christ. Its aim is to replace the true God. Its works and purposes are all directed towards that end. The devil works behind the scenes to accomplish its aims. The secrecy of its moves is designed to defeat the promises of God's Word. As a spirit being, it marshals its powers to intervene and interrupt the order and harmony of God's creation. The devil is the cause behind disastrous storms and catastrophes. It is the cause behind massive confusion. It is the force that works destruction and death. But, the devil is a limited spirit being whose evil workings our Lord Jesus Christ has exposed. The devil appeared to Jesus in the

Judean wilderness and sought to defeat the Savior of the world by its sorted temptations. The authority of God's Word, pronounced by Jesus, thwarted the devil's efforts. His command was "get you hence Satan."

I John 3:8b

For this purpose the son of God was manifested, that he might destroy the works of the devil.

Praise God, we are no longer subjected to this evil spirit's devices nor should we ever fear its power. When we resist this evil spirit it will flee! In the next topic we will begin to review satanic doctrines.

POSSESSION OR CHOICE

Destiny, predestination, fate, fortune, luck, and chance are all deterministic doctrines. These doctrinal beliefs undermine our freedom of choice. All of these concepts have become a playground in which Satan works its devices. For insistence, the word destiny is a "trickster" word. Its modern-day meaning shadows and conceals the force responsible for determining the end result in a given matter. The description of "who" it is that is responsible for the action in this word remains unnamed and even masked by obscurity. This unnamed sinister force is left to the surmising of those who are hearing the word. It is the masked obscured force in the modern meaning of destiny that makes room for the devil to operate its intentions. When the implied power in the meaning of destiny is fully named then we are able to grasp its deviant, idolatrous, meaning. The fundamental lie

121

embraced within the concept of destiny is that the individual's effort, energy, and discipline are not the controlling power in one's life. The highest controlling power remains that unseen force out there; it is the ultimate cause bringing a blessing or a cursing, its destiny that does it. Lies, lies, and more lies; but we know better! We have become wise to the true meaning implied in the word destiny.

The next word we will examine is predestinate. The Bible does use the word predestinate. Any valid discussion about the meaning of this word must take into consideration the predestinator. Because God is all-knowing, His view of eternity precedes the beginning and the end. His foreknowledge precedes our choices. He does not determine our choices; however, He knows, in advance, what we will choose. The outstanding problem people have with the word "predestinate" comes from mistakenly associating it with the concept of destiny. Within the concept of destiny a supposed god, or some unknown force, always does the choosing, and then casts its decision upon human life. The word "predestinate", is used four times in the Bible and it never refers to God's determining anything apart from our ability to choose.

The word "fate" is often referred to as a power of determination. This supposed power exists somewhere in the heavens but hovers beyond our sight. It is said to possess the uncanny ability to act upon us by overstepping our ability to determine our future. This, supposed, great power of determination cancels out our freedom of will and we have no choice; we must submit to it. According to its popular concept fate's power literally takes away our freedom to act. The idea of fate, however, stands in opposition to freedom of will. All of these weird ideas are precepts associated with fate.

The Christian believer should have no problem recognizing the doctrines that surround the idea of fate. We must not be taken in and deceived by false theologies. To do so will rob us of both our power and our peace. False theologies are always floating around and they are designed to blind and deceive. However, to walk in fellowship with God brings great joy, peace, and power. By manifesting the power and love of God, we can walk victoriously over the "wiles of the devil" and any lying doctrine that seeks to verify the meaning of fate. We are not going to be "taken in" by every wind of false doctrines!

Next we will look into the concept of luck. The fundamental claim about luck is its power. Far too many people believe in luck's power to bring benefits and bestow blessings; that it can supply needs and wants. They also believe the power of luck can bring harm to their lives. All these claims add up to something of great importance if they are factual. If the assertions made about luck are true, then we have an exalted "god force" operating in and about us. The design of luck theology is purposefully crafted to refute the abiding reality of God and the sure promises of His Word. Demented teachings about the "luck god" are designed to rob our Heavenly Father of the praise and honor He is due.

Luck is not an inexplicable force that cannot be understood, explained, or accounted for. Neither is it a source of prosperity; nor is it the cause of evil and destruction. That is the workmanship of the devil. Neither is luck the source of happenstance. To confess luck is an idolatrous confession. It is a misguided belief in the existence of a metaphysical god. It is also a denial of cause and effect. A confession

123

of luck is passive submission to fatalistic thinking. Luck is a doctrine of devils that stands diametrically opposed to the living Word of God!

The last of these deceiver words we are going to review is the word chance. The design of our Creator does not include the operation of chance; not even on a microscopic level. Thusly, there is no right response to chance, for chance does not exist. Chance does not fit within the context of purpose. God has built order and harmony throughout the universe. A sheep behaves like a sheep. A duck behaves like a duck. They were created to behave in a precise manner. Our massive planet Earth continues to revolve around the Sun with just enough tilting back and forth to make our changing seasons an unchanging certainty.

God built order and harmony into the very fabric of life. We can count on the constant order and processes that make life work. Sunshine and rain, seedtime and harvest, are a sure constant; and gravity is always there. The air we breathe is there, praise God! Water to satisfy our thirst is always there. What are the chances of all this changing? Anyone can see the concept of chance just does not fit into biological and physical spheres of order and harmony. Nor does chance fit into the functioning of spiritual realities. What a wonderful creation God has made and none of this order is subject to chance.

The concept of chance seeks to exclude the operation of God's presence in our daily lives. It is, however, by His power that we live and move and have our being. We can cast the thoughts of our hearts upon Him; there our hearts will be safe. We can cast our cares upon

Him for He cares for us. Here is a great truth all of us need to understand. Just no category in life is outside of God's care, God's power, and God's love. No matter how big the need you may have, God is big enough to take care of it. No matter how big the failure and sin, God is big enough to cleanse you. No matter how incurable the disease God is big enough to heal you. No matter how heavy your heart's burden God's comfort is big enough to make it light. If life looks hopeless to you, God is still big enough. He is the God of promise and hope. He is God almighty! So what do you need in your life? God is always big enough. God has left nothing to chance!

TRANSGENDER LIES

Earlier we examined the absurd practice called sex change. The devil is actively working to make sex change an accepted practice. Lies about its normality, and its acceptance by society, are evil, devilish, ploys. It is a lying, devilish, doctrine that an individual can change their gender from a man to a woman or a woman to a man. Nonetheless, the infestation of devilish lies has infected the gullible minds of individuals seeking to change their sex. It is plainly obvious that those choosing to have a sex operation are opposing themselves. They are casting away their God-given endowment and slipping into the entrapment of a fantasy world. The strangely, queered, motivations of those who are traveling this pathway need to be brought to light. That they have a gender identity problem is in fact their patsy misnomer terminology for a selfish, twisted, ungodly, desire. For many of them, the problem by which they are overwhelmed is devil spirit possession.

The perversions they are adopting need to be lovingly, but sternly confronted. When they choose to have deliverance from devil spirits they can be set free.

Men are designed to be men and a man's counterpart is the woman. By the way, it is an impossibility to change one's DNA. God did not intend that a man or a woman should attempt to change their given design. As a matter of fact, it is impossible for them to do so! Sex change is against the established order of God's design. He has never made a gender mix-up mistake. It is the misdirected attempts of men and women who are seeking to change their God-given bodies; that are the mistake.

Gender change procedures have left a trail of misery upon those who have undergone the operation. The medical personnel who are accommodating the delusions, and sorted desires, of their patients, need to stop what they are practicing upon these people. They need to refuse to accommodate the deranged, misguided, desires of the individuals who have chosen to butcher their God-given endowment. Why are they accommodating evil? Maybe some of these wayward surgeons need to endure a stay in prison in order to clear up their thinking.

Parental failure to correct the freakish, unnatural, desires of their children is an indictment against the parent's sanity and also their morality. They have failed to help their offspring develop soundness in their thinking. Those parents who have allowed this corrupted judgment to take root and grow in the minds of their sons and daughters are behaving more like criminals than caring parents. They are proving themselves to be spiritually corrupt. No stable-minded parent would allow this weird, devilish, behavior to fester and grow in the minds and hearts of their children.

The bewildering illusion that sex change is available is indeed a devilish lie. It is in fact not attainable. It is only a devilish ploy. To claim that it's available is substantiating a devilish doctrine. Those who are participating in this practice need to wake up to the reality of its harmful outcomes.

THE CLIMATE CHANGE HOAX

By this time, surely, we have sharpened our spiritual perception and awareness. Our understanding of spiritual matters qualifies us to recognize and identify devilish doctrines. We addressed the disastrous climate change doctrine earlier. The lively debate about climate change continues to occupy center stage in our modern-day society. A large segment of our population has bought into the dubious concept. They think it is real and they support it!

Earlier we looked at the motives behind what climate change proponents are proclaiming. The government of the United States has bought into the climate change hoax. They have enacted laws and regulations that are adversely affecting the citizenry of our land. Just a casual look reveals how some governmental officials and their backers are prospering by the platforms and regulations they have enacted. Educational institutions have indoctrinated their students into accepting the bogus belief concerning climate change. They fall in line and teach environmental threats because they are fearful of losing the money the government supplies. The news media have brainwashed the general public into believing that the climate change doctrine is factual. They are fast to quote scientific research that may be completely unfounded. However, the media lost the trust of the public years ago. We know their true motive is making a profit.

Our examination of this highly charged issue must absolutely be viewed from a spiritual perspective. Without the dimension of the spiritual view, seriously false conclusions are leading to disastrous consequences. We are already witnessing how destructive this doctrine has become. Climate change advocates have failed to include what the Word of God proclaims. Their narratives have left out what God has to say about the climate.

The everlasting covenant God has established with the Earth, and the people in it, is ongoing. It's still in affect; it will not cease. His promise remains:

Genesis 8:22

While the earth remains, seedtime and harvest, and cold and heat, and summer and winter, and day and night shall not cease.

So, now the question has become whose word are you going to believe? Will you believe the trustworthy Word of our loving Heavenly Father, the Creator of Heaven and Earth; or will you believe the words of men who have imagined vain things? False scientific theories and findings cannot negate the order and standing of God Almighty. Human extinction is not within the care and keeping of Earth's people. It is true, people are often destructive, but ultimately it's God's timetable that will bring the end to pass.

God is in control of Earth's keeping. The end time of the Earth, as we know it, is clearly defined in the Scriptures. Nowhere does Scripture teach that human existence will be smothered out by a lack of oxygen. Again, the fervent heat destruction of the Earth referred to in Scripture comes after the millennial (1,000 years) reign of the Lord Jesus Christ and not before. The sequences of end-time events are clearly defined in the Bible! Proof positive that climate change is a hoax; that it is a false, devilish, doctrine, is that it contradicts the Bible record concerning when Earth will cease to be.

ARE THE DEAD ALIVE AND IN HEAVEN?

The mistaken assumption that the dead are alive and in heaven lingers on and on in the minds of many Christians. However, this assumption contradicts what the Bible teaches. It is because of what the Bible teaches about this subject that we have a clear and accurate understanding of the state of the dead. There are no other sourcebooks that teach the heavenly perspective about this subject. So, in affect, we have what men and women have to say about the state of the dead in open contrast to what God has to say. The smart choice is what God has to say.

I Thessalonians 4:13-17

But I would not have you to be ignorant, brethren, concerning them which are asleep,(dead) that you sorrow not, even as others which have no hope. For if we believe that Jesus died and rose again, even so, them also which sleep (are dead) in Jesus will God bring with Him. For this we say unto you by the word of the Lord, that we which are alive and remain unto the coming of the Lord, shall not prevent (that is precede) them which are asleep (dead). For the Lord Himself shall descend from heaven with a shout, with the voice of the archangel, and with the trump of God: and the dead in Christ shall rise first:
Then we which are alive, and remain, shall be caught up together with them in the clouds, to meet the Lord in the air: and so, shall we ever be with the Lord.

The clarity of I Thessalonians 4:13-17 teaches us that the dead remain dead until the Lord Jesus Christ resurrects them to newness of life. The word "sleep" in the above Scripture passage is used as a synonym for dead. Sleep is meant to be a more comforting word than dead. In sleep, there is no consciousness. The same is true concerning the dead. The dead are without memory and therefore without consciousness. They will remain in that state of unconsciousness until they are resurrected by the command of the Lord Jesus Christ. Then (and not until then) they will be raised with incorruptible new bodies and will have regained consciousness.

The clear words of the above Scripture are "the Lord himself shall descend from heaven and the dead in Christ shall rise first" and those still alive on Earth "shall be caught up together with them (with the Dead) in the clouds to meet the Lord in the air." The emphatic truth of these verses is stated so plainly that no one needs to miss it. The dead will get to Heaven when Jesus Christ calls them to everlasting life.

1 Corinthians 15:42-44

So also is the resurrection of the dead. It is sown in corruption; it is raised in incorruption: It is sown in dishonor; it is raised in glory: It Is sown in weakness; it is raised in power: It is sown a natural body; it is raised a spiritual body. There is a natural body, and there is a spiritual body.

Fake science has opened up the demented category of spiritualism. The devilish doctrine that "the dead are alive now" is straight from Satan's tool chest. Satan can and does counterfeit phenomenon that appears to be genuine. In seances and other "hookie-pook" activities like extrasensory perception activity, devilish powers counterfeit the dead and can make them appear to be alive. The unsuspecting, and gullible, hold on to these delusions and believe them to be true. The reality is, this kind of activity adds up to the devilish doctrine "that the dead are alive." Christian believers need to rise up and steer clear of this devilish entrapment. The devil's tricky devices will become obvious when God's people turn on their spiritual perception and awareness. They must depend upon the accuracy of God's living Word of truth for the right answers that they seek.

THE DOCTRINE OF THE TRINITY

Questions surrounding the validity of the Trinity doctrine have been voiced since the third century AD. Christian believers have remained divided by this doctrine up to the present day. The idea of Jesus Christ being co-equal with God gained support early in the 4th century. Bishop Alexander, of Alexandria Egypt, along with other bishops, claimed that God can do anything He chooses, so God incarnated Himself – He became human. He chose to become Jesus. They believe that only if Jesus was fully human could he atone for human sin and only if he was fully divine could he have the power to save us. Arius, a priest, also from Alexandria Egypt, believed that God adopted Jesus as His son, but that did not mean they were equal. He believed that Jesus of Nazareth was a real man, not some divine aberration of God, or God, for that matter.

The Roman emperor Constantine convened the Council of Nicaea in 325 AD with the expectation of developing unity among the hundreds of independent bishops ruling the Christian Community at that time. At the emperor's behest, the council pinned the doctrine Constantine wanted. However, their doctrine of the Trinity failed to produce unity. What it did foster was divisions, hatred, and even savage murders. The emperor, having intervened in a religious debate, made it possible for the bishops, standing with him, to levy political power. It is not that those militant bishops were more qualified to define the identity of Christ. However, with the power of the emperor at their disposal, they could force their views upon dissenters. They set out to thwart any opposition to their dogmatic stance. The council's conclusion stated that "Jesus Christ was very God of very God." Now, having the power of the emperor backing them up, militant bishops began to war against the opposing bishops who would not comply with the council's conclusion. They immediately banished Arius.

It wasn't that the dissenters against the council's conclusion were pagan God-rejecters. They were, in fact, brethren with a different belief about the person of Christ. They were not militants, wheeling their swords of righteousness. Actually, this is a closer description of those who supported the council's decision. The vehement attitudes they displayed against their brethren are clearly an indication that they were not, in fact, qualified to decide the true nature of Christ's identity.

Those who deny that Jesus Christ is God have their own set of doctrinal beliefs. They are sometimes referred to as Biblical Unitarians. First and foremost, they believe God is one God and is not divided into three distinct Gods. They believe God created a seed in the womb of Mary. That's when the promised Messiah developed to become the only begotten Son of God (no pre-existence). They believe Jesus was a true man born with perfect blood. He was as human as Adam. He was never contaminated by sin. He walked perfectly before his Heavenly Father. The spirit of God was given to him in full measure. Through obedience, Jesus became the perfect sacrifice for the sins of the world. In obedience to his Heavenly Father, he suffered death on a Roman cross. God raised him from the dead after three days and three nights. Today, he is in Heaven and is seated at God's right hand. Biblical Unitarians, just like Trinitarians, are staunch in their beliefs.

The devilish controversy over the identity of Jesus is a crippling testimony still churning and stirring within the Christian Community. It has separated the Body of Christ into hard-hearted divisions. It has robbed the church of its unity and its strength. Arguments among brethren over the meaning of certain Scriptures seem to go on and on. Diverse interpretations continue to stoke the fires of division. To resolve the critical issues between them both sides need to measure up to what the Word of God teaches about the relationship between Christian brethren. Creating discord among Christian brethren is a common tool utilized by satanic powers. Divisions, suspicions, condemnation, the withdrawal of fellowship, and thinking evil among Christians; all of this needs to cease. Please, replace those negative attitudes with compassion, open arms of forgiveness, preferring others before oneself, being tenderhearted, and loving each other with the love of God. It is the absence of all these uplifting qualities that invite Satan's intervention into the ongoing Trinitarian controversy.

Centuries of the debate have never settled the controversy; surely it's time for something better. It is time that Christian brethren take an altogether different approach to questions surrounding this Church doctrines. Their attitude and behavior needs to reflect tolerance, friendship, understanding, patience, benevolence, and brotherly love toward each other. Please, please, exhibit these! God is not, and will never be, pleased with a division among Christian believers. Unity and sanctification please Him. Heaven's door is open to Trinitarian Christians and it is also open to Non-Trinitarian Christians. The standard for entrance into heaven is to be born-again of God's spirit. Doctrinal beliefs are formulated by men and women. When their doctrines are founded upon truth they will endure. Those that are predicated upon error eventually fall to the ground and fade away.

Prayer for your Trinitarian brethren by Unitarians, and prayer for your Unitarian brethren by Trinitarians, will bring about wonderful change. The unity of heart-felt prayers will open doors of opportunity to minister to those with the meekness to receive. God's guidance will give just the right answers for healing and deliverance to take place. God will reward our efforts with victory after victory. He will unlock doors that have been shut far too long. The hangover of a dark controversy between Christian brothers must be replaced with graceful reconciliation. This is an obtainable goal. Nothing short of loving grace, and unity of heart, can please our Heavenly Father. Merciful, peaceful, loving, words between us can get the job done. There is no need for delay. We can place our arguments to one side and sow a new crop of seed; one that will bring about the healing that is needed. Revival in our attitudes about each other will carry us to the peaceful place of unity and holiness.

Made in the USA
Columbia, SC
09 October 2023

23918572R00088